COPING WITH

A

Drug-Abusing
Parent

Lawrence Clayton, Ph.D.

THE ROSEN PUBLISHING GROUP, INC./NEW YORK

Published in 1991, 1995 by The Rosen Publishing Group, Inc.
29 East 21st Street, New York, NY 10010

Revised Edition *1995*

Library of Congress Cataloging-in-Publication Data
Clayton. L. (Lawrence)
  Coping with a drug abusing parent/Lawrence Clayton.
    p.   cm.
  Includes bibliographical references and index.
  Summary: Describes drug addiction, its symptoms and manifestations: the effect of an addict on his or her family: how to handle the pressures of living with an addict: and how to get help.
  ISBM 0-8239-1950-1
  1. Children of narcotic addicts—United States—Juvenile literature. 2. Children—United States—Drug use—Juvenile literature. 3. Narcotic addicts—United States—Family relationships—Juvenile literature.   4. Codependence (Psychology)—United States—Juvenile literature.   [1. Drug abuse.]   I. title.
HV5824.C45C53   1991
362.29'13—dc20   90-24855
                                                        CIP
                                                         AC

Manufactured in the United States of America

To:
Frank Drukin,
a great and loyal friend,
who served with me in Vietnam
I'll never forget you!

ABOUT THE AUTHOR ◇

Lawrence Clayton grew up in the small town of Austin, in central Nevada. There he learned "from the inside out" about life in an alcoholic family and about coping with a drug-abusing parent. His stepfather was an alcoholic who drank himself to death. His step-brother was an addict who committed suicide. His uncle, also an alcoholic, was likewise a victim of suicide. Lawrence finally escaped this situation by joining the United States Army when he was seventeen. He served three years in Germany and two years in Vietnam.

Dr. Clayton earned a Bachelor's Degree from Texas Wesleyan College (summa cum laude), a Master's Degree from Texas Christian University, and a Doctorate from Texas Woman's University.

Since 1971 he has treated children, youth, and families as an ordained minister specializing in pastoral counseling. He holds certifications in Marriage and Family Therapy and Drug and Alcohol Counseling. He founded and directs the Oklahoma Family Institute in Oklahoma City. Much of his work is with children from homes in which alcohol and other drugs have played a significant role.

He is an Approved Supervisor for the American Association for Marriage and Family Therapy.

Dr. Clayton is the author of numerous other books, including *Assessment and Management of the Suicidal Adolescent, Coping with Depression, Coping with Being Gifted, Coping with a Learning Disability, Coping with*

v

Sports Injuries, Careers in Psychology, and *Coping with Phobias.* He also serves as an Associate Editor for the journal *Family Perspective.*

He lives in Piedmont, Oklahoma, with his wife, Cathy, and their children, Rebecca, Larry, and Amy.

Contents

CHAPTER 1

The Drug-Abusing Parent: Promises and Reality

*J*ames was excited. He could hardly wait to see his father. It had been so long since the separation. He could still remember his father standing in the yard of the old house as his mother backed the car out of the driveway for the last time. He had leaned out the window, waved to his father, and shouted "I love you, Dad!"

"I love you, too, son!" his father had hollered back, "I'll come to see you as soon as I handle this." Then, pointing to his mother, he yelled, 'I love you, too, babe. I'll come for both of you just as soon as I'm straightened out."

After crying for miles, they rode along quietly. It was after dark when James broke the silence with the question that was tormenting both of them, "Will he come for us, Mamma? Will he?"

"I don't know, honey," she had said. Then, considering it a little more deeply, she added, "I think he will if he can ever get straightened out."

That had been almost two years ago. "Straightened out!" he repeated aloud. "I wonder if he really meant it?"

"Who are you talking to, James?" asked Mrs. Rhoades, his fourth-grade English teacher.

"No one," he said. "I'm sorry, I wasn't thinking."

"Oh, you were thinking all right," she said. "But not about your poetry assignment. You were day-dreaming. Want to tell me about it?"

"My dad is coming to see me," he said excitedly. Then the words came so fast that Mrs. Rhoades could hardly understand him. "I haven't seen him since Mom and I left Portland. He's picking me up after school. Mom left for the weekend. Dad and I are going to spend the whole weekend together. He's taking me to the Braves' game, then we're going to the new amusement park."

"Okay," she said. "Slow down. No wonder you're having trouble writing poetry. Put your things away and go get ready to see your dad."

"Oh, thanks, Mrs. Rhoades!" he said, as he ran out the door and down the hall to his locker.

Three hours later, Mrs. Rhoades finished grading papers and preparing for Monday's class. She grabbed her briefcase and went to check her mailbox in the school office for messages. There she found a single sheet of paper: "James Miller's father called. Said he was sorry, but something's come up. He'll make it some other time."

"Oh, no!" she said aloud. "Where could James be?" She ran out of the building "James!" she called. "James, where are you?" There seemed to be no one anywhere around the school. "James!" she shouted as she ran by the old gym. "James, please answer me!" She was getting frightened. What if some one had taken him? "James!" she shouted even louder. She had just decided to call the police when she caught a glimpse of something yellow just visible over the back of the bus stop bench. "Could that be James's yellow raincoat?" she wondered as she ran to the bench. It was, and there was James sound asleep on the bench.

"James?" she said quietly. "Wake up."

He sat up and looked at her. "My dad isn't coming, is he?"

"No, James, he isn't," she said. "I don't know what happened. The note just said something had come up. But it also said he would make it some other time."

"No, he won't," James said angrily. "I know Dad. He must have started snortin' cocaine again. Otherwise he'd have been here. He's never comin' to get me." Suddenly, he began to cry, big, deep sobs.

She sat down on the bench and held him. She'd never heard a child cry like this. It was as if someone had died. He cried for almost an hour. All she could do was hold him. When he was finished, she said, "I guess you'll just have to come home with me. Do you have any idea where your mother is?"

"No, but her answering service can find her," he said.

"Let's go into the school," she said. "We can call the answering service from there. We'll tell them your mother can pick you up at my house. Is that okay?" Without a word, he gave assent by getting up and taking her hand. Slowly, they walked to the front of the school.

"Hey, I think that's Mom's car," he said. "The white one parked at the curb."

Just then, they heard her scream, "James!" Turning, they saw her running toward them from the far side of *the school, "Oh, thank God," she said as she hugged him desperately. "I was afraid I'd lost you, too!"*

She stood there hugging him and crying, wishing she hadn't said that word. She had meant to tell him later when they were alone, but it was too late. He was too bright and too sensitive, and he knew her too well. Her stomach churned, dreading the storm that she knew was about to break.

He pushed back just enough to see her face. "Too?" he asked.

She tried not to answer him. She looked pleadingly at the teacher as if begging her somehow to make this terrible truth go away.

"Too?" he literally shouted the question at her. Now he was shaking her, demanding an answer. "Too?"

The color had drained from her face. Between sobs she said, "police called . . . answering service . . . heart attack . . . they tried to save him . . . bad drugs . . . dead."

"Oh, no," said Mrs. Rhoades as the truth hit her.

James screamed, "No!" and tried to run. "No! I want my daddy. He can't be dead! It's a mistake! He said he'd come to get me! He said so!"

His mother refused to let him go, and shaking her head from side to side, she cried out, "No mistake."

James let out a strange whimpering sound, fell to the ground, and lay motionless. He had fainted.

Mrs. Rhoades helped her pick him up. Together, they carried him into the teacher's lounge, put him on the couch, and covered him with a blanket.

"I'll get you some tea," Mrs. Rhoades said to his mother.

Later, as they sat on the other couch, his mother told her the rest of the story. "In college, James's father was a good athlete and a good student. We married and had planned to attend medical school together after gradua-

tion. Even with being pregnant, giving birth, and taking care of James, I made it. He was expelled because of drugs."

Shaking her head, she almost whispered, "He made our lives miserable. He just couldn't leave the drugs alone. When we left, he promised James he would get straightened out and come to see him. He called last week to say he had done it. He wanted us to be a family again. I wanted him to spend time with James first. There wasn't a single day in those two years that James didn't ask about him."

Many readers will be able to identify with James's story. It happens every day. Hard to believe? According to the National Institute on Drug Abuse, 583,038 people in the United States died because of addictive substances during 1992. That's over one person every minute.

And if those figures are not horrifying enough, the average age of those who died was thirty-eight. That means that most of them were someone's parent. And most of them, like James's father, made their family's lives miserable for many years before death intervened. And it almost always does—fully 93 percent of those who are addicted die as result!

Dr. David Olms calls this a "national disgrace," because we have the ability to treat drug abusers successfully. He adds that "with treatment, approximately 90 per cent will achieve full recovery."

CHAPTER 2

Drug Abuse: Fact and Fiction

Melanie remembers watching Sam pull a marijuana cigarette out of his coat pocket and snicker as he showed it to his friend John. They were sitting across the aisle from her in the last row on the school bus. They glanced at her and didn't seem to mind that she was watching as they lit it and passed it back and forth between them.

Phil came home early from his Boy Scout meeting to find his older brother Rob standing at their father's bar with a whiskey bottle in one hand and the teapot in the other. Rob started yelling at him for borrowing his headphones. That really surprised Phil, because Rob had never seemed to mind before. He decided not to ask Rob why he was pouring tea into the whiskey bottle.

Marsha has been selling drugs to her friends at school for two years now. An adult friend named

Reggie meets her in the parking lot on her lunch break. Marsha usually starts by giving a hit of speed or LSD to friends at a party. Gradually, as they want more and more, she begins charging them.

Scott's Uncle Harry has been arrested often for driving drunk. Each time Uncle Harry calls Scott's mother to come and get him out. She always gets upset and cries a lot, but she does it. Scott's father becomes very angry when he discovers that his wife has paid Uncle Harry's fine and bailed him out again. Their fights are beginning to worry Scott.

We all know someone who uses drugs. It's just a sad fact of life these days—they're everywhere.

But what is the difference between someone who uses, or abuses, drugs and someone who is addicted to drugs?

And what if that someone is one of your parents?

To understand addiction, it is important to look at some of the myths that keep people confused about addiction and what it is—and isn't.

Myth #1. All "real" alcoholics and addicts are skid-row bums whose families and employers have long ago given up on them.

Fact. Less than one tenth of one percent of all addicts live on skid row. Most of the rest live with their families and go to work every day. To outsiders their lives appear quite normal.

Case Study: John is an electrical engineer. He has worked for the Alpha Company for fifteen years. He has been married to Phyllis for twenty-one years, and they have four children.

John started drinking beer when he was thirteen. At

first he drank only on weekends, and then only a couple of cans of beer each day. By the time he was fifteen he was drinking a six-pack every Saturday and Sunday. When he was seventeen he was drinking a six-pack several times a week and as much as a case of beer on weekends.

Phyllis met John at a party in college. She was impressed with his ability to handle his liquor. That first night John drank at least ten cans of beer and a pint of whiskey and never appeared to be drunk. It wasn't long until they were going steady and partying every weekend.

After graduation John enrolled in engineering school and Phyllis got a job. Within three months Phyllis was pregnant. Her doctor told her that the parties would have to stop. When she told John, he seemed elated about the pregnancy but somewhat upset about the parties. Still, he promised to quit.

Within a week he came home very late and very drunk. Once again, he promised to stop. He didn't, but Phyllis was too happy with the prospect of her first baby to be very concerned. Soon John graduated from engineering school, got a promising job, and their future looked bright.

Ten years later they had four children and John was chief engineer of the company and president of the administrative board at their church. He was also drinking a quart of whiskey every Friday, Saturday, and Sunday.

This family live in an affluent neighborhood and drive expensive cars. And all four of the children are beginning to show, to some degree, the scars of children of alcoholics.

John is an alcoholic; that is, he is addicted to alcohol. Addiction is defined as *the loss of ability to control one's use of a mood-altering substance or behavior*.

Myth #2. People *become* alcoholics or addicts.

Fact. While it is possible for some people to become alcoholic or addicted by using alcohol or drugs for many years, for others it's much easier. They are born with a genetic "code" that sets them up to become addicted.

In that way, addiction is similar to diabetes. People who are diabetic are born with a specific gene that at a certain age will make that person diabetic.

Everyone's brain contains many chemicals. Some of them are called endorphin, encaplin, dopamine, and serotonin. These brain chemicals have been called "Mother Nature's morphines." They are a built-in, natural high. They give us a sense of peace and well-being. These chemicals are released into the brain at various times—after exercise, when we see a beautiful painting, when our team wins, when a person of the opposite sex tells us we're cute.

When a person with a genetic predisposition toward addiction uses drugs or drinks, his or her body turns a portion of the alcohol or drug into something called THIQ. THIQ is a suppressor chemical; it suppresses endorphin, encaplin, dopamine, and serotonin.

The more drugs an addict uses, the more THIQ is produced. While temporarily making him feel better, the drug is also causing a by-product that will, in the end, make him feel worse. He will continue using because the drug makes him feel better—temporarily until more THIQ is produced.

When a person without the genetic predisposition toward addiction uses drugs or drinks, his or her body breaks down the alcohol or drug into substances that the body uses or expels. If this person continues to use drugs or drink alcohol long enough, his or her brain will begin to produce THIQ.

Eventually all alcoholics or addicts must drink or use

not just to feel better or get high, but to feel normal—the way most of us do every day. That is why an alcoholic or addict is always one drink or one dose short.

(Although research has yet to validate it completely, this same process is probably also at work in the brains of all people who are addicted to behaviors such as shopaholics, workaholics, and churchaholics. Research has validated the process in the brains of compulsive gamblers).

Case Study: The first time Bob smoked pot he was fourteen. He really liked the "rush" he got. He felt euphoric—"high" and very happy and pleased with life and himself in general. At first a couple of hits a day from a joint (marijuana cigarette) were enough.

Within a year he was smoking an entire joint each evening. By the time he entered college he was smoking several joints a day. When he was twenty-five, Bob was lacing (adding) THC (a stronger drug) into each joint. At forty, Bob was smoking crack (a very potent form of cocaine). This is a condition called *tolerance*. Tolerance is a sign that a user is addicted and that THIQ is being produced in ever greater amounts. Graphically, addiction looks like this:

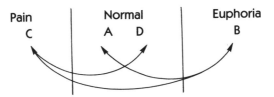

Before Bob started using, he was experiencing a normal mood (point A). When he used the first time, he got a euphoric "rush" (point B). Because of THIQ, he eventually was in pain whenever he wasn't using (point C). Finally,

Bob was using just to feel normal (point D). That was when Bob began to use more and stronger drugs.

Note: A word of warning is needed. Even though Bob's tolerance for drugs is increasing (that is, he is able to use more and more), he is moving closer and closer to the point at which the drugs will kill him. *There is only one difference between a drug and a poison, and that is the quantity.* Any drug that will alter your mood will also kill you if used in large enough quantity.

Myth #3. Addicts lose control every time they use.

Fact. Addicts can control their use for limited periods of time. In fact, alcoholics and addicts often do without alcohol or drugs for a time to prove to themselves or others that they are not addicted. But they are in pain during this time, and they want to use or drink. The only valid "proof" is being able to stop using, not miss the drug, and not start again. In such a case the person is truly not addicted and will find other ways to enjoy life naturally.

Case Study: Oscar found himself using more and more speed. He started when he was driving a truck coast to coast. All the other drivers used it to help them stay awake. He justified the use of speed by telling himself that he was a safer driver. But now it seemed that he was always using, and he felt terrible when he wasn't.

Somewhere in a far corner of his mind was the nagging question, "Could I be addicted?" He had to know, so he decided to test himself. He would quit for a week. It was Monday, and he was determined.

By Tuesday he was "coming down," and he felt terrible. Wednesday he slept all day. Thursday and Friday were horrible; he felt as if his head were about to explode, and he was shaking all over.

Friday night he tried to watch television. By midnight he was in a bar drinking. "At least," he thought, "I'm not addicted to speed." Or was he? On Sunday he was using again. He had successfully lied to himself—until he found that his son, Oliver, eighteen and an honors student in his freshman year at the state university, was using speed to stay up all night and study.

Oscar's first reaction was fury, but his son convinced him that he, Oliver, was not addicted either. The speed was just "useful"—it made him a better student, helped him keep his scholarship.

Oscar calmed down and accepted the explanation. Okay, both of them were all right. They weren't addicted. They just "used" now and then when it helped them.

But far below his conscious mind Oscar realized that something wasn't right, that he and his son were skating on thin ice. Still, he refused to face the fact that he was addicted.

Remember, the worst lies addicts ever tell are the ones they tell themselves.

Myth #4. Once people are addicted to alcohol, they drink until they pass out.

Fact. Some alcoholics are able to have one or two drinks and then quit—on occasion. *But an alcoholic can never be sure that he or she will be able to have one or two drinks and then stop.*

Case Study: June had decided to cut down on alcohol. Lately, she had been worried about some of the things she had done while she was drinking.

June worked in sales with several other people, and it had become a habit for them to stop off at a bar for a couple of drinks after work. Tuesday was no exception. But this time June had two margueritas and excused herself with, "I have a husband and two kids at home. See you later."

June's husband, Cecil, and their sons Tony and Kile were happy to see her come home the same time as other working mothers in the neighborhood. They were impressed when she told them that things were going to be different from now on. Impressed—but not quite believing. They'd heard it before. "From now on I'll be home every night by 6:30!" was greeted with an enthusiasm that was, shall we say, restrained. But, true to her word, June was home by 6:30 on Wednesday and again on Thursday. Even on Friday she managed to make it by 7 o'clock.

The weekend was uneventful, except that June's disposition steadily became worse. By Sunday afternoon she had screamed at everyone in her family, two neighbors, her mother—she had even kicked the dog!

On Monday evening the family went about their business at home very quietly, dreading what might happen. But June was home, and by 6:30 p.m.

On Tuesday she stopped off with her friends from work again, and this time she was swept out with the dust when the bar closed at two o'clock in the morning. On the way home she was arrested for driving under the influence. It was her third DUI and carried the very real possibility of a stiff prison sentence. Her children were terrified of that.

Myth #5. You're not an addict if you use only on weekends.

Fact. Addicts are of at least four types. One is the daily user. This type of addict may use all day long or only in the evenings. He may get very high or just stay tipsy for hours.

Another is the binge addict. A binge addict uses mostly on weekends and holidays, but no matter when he uses, he gets loaded almost every time.

Note: Daily addicts are easier to help than binge addicts. That is because a binge addict is accustomed to periods of abstinence followed by periods of drunkenness. The fact that a binge addict is straight adds nothing new to his pattern of use, whereas being sober is a new experience for the daily addict.

Case Study: Joe and Jeff are brothers. Both of them are addicts. Recently both of them entered treatment. Joe was the daily user type; Jeff was a binge addict. From the beginning the treatment staff noticed how different they were.

Joe went into severe withdrawal when he quit using. His body wasn't used to being without drugs. Jeff had no problem being without drugs, at least not for the first week. His body was used to being without drugs for extended periods of time.

After Joe got past his withdrawal symptoms, he was very cooperative and did well in the treatment program. Jeff was cooperative from the first day, but he craved drugs every weekend.

Both Joe and Jeff were discharged after thirty days of treatment. Joe never used again. Jeff managed to stay straight for two months. He has been in treatment five times since then, each time characterized by a period of abstinence followed by a relapse.

Myth #6. There is no difference in how genetic addiction affects men and women.

Fact. One type of genetic addiction is passed from either mother or father to son or daughter. It is characterized by a later and slower developing addiction. Another type is passed only from father to son and is characterized by early and excessive use and violent behavior.

Case Study: Donald and Larry were both fourteen. They liked to hang out together and they liked to drink together. There was a problem, however.

Donald seemed to get angry every time he drank. He seemed to become agitated much more often. Some of his behaviors frightened Larry—like the time he had beaten up their friend Tony. Larry found himself "walking on eggshells" around Donald's anger, afraid to upset him. It seemed to Larry that Donald could explode any time.

Finally, Larry started making excuses not to be around when Donald was drinking. That was when Donald turned on him, called him names, and threatened to kill him. Funny? Maybe not! Larry believed him.

A few nights later when Donald was drunk, he got into a fight with his mother. He stabbed her to death.

Myth #7. My parents' addiction is their problem. It won't affect my life after I grow up because I'll never use drugs.

Fact. When parents are addicted, everyone in the family is affected by it. The consequences of growing up in an addicted home can and usually do last a lifetime. The problems are so pervasive, so much a part of a child's personality and emotional pattern, that they can be passed down through several generations.

Even though you may never drink or use, your parents' addiction could cause problems that would make life difficult for your grandchildren!

Case Study: Marsha had always hated her father's using. Before it got so bad, they were a happy family—like a sitcom on TV! Now Dad was hardly ever home, and when he was, she wished that he weren't. There was no love in her family anymore. Her father was seriously depressed.

His angry outbursts were bad enough, but then the sexual abuse started, nights of terror when she lay rigid and listened as footsteps approached her room, days when she felt tormented by guilt, blame, and anger and tried to think what to do.

She believed that it was partly her fault and partly the result of her father's using. She promised herself that she would never marry anyone who used and that she would protect her children from anything like what she had suffered.

When Marsha was eighteen she met Cal. He seemed just right for her: He was very religious and was planning to become a minister. He never used and was strongly against drugs. They went together for two and a half years. When Cal graduated from the seminary, they were married. Fourteen months later their first child was born. They named her Sarah.

Cal was dedicated to the Lord. He was determined. They were happy—almost. The problem? Cal was upset with his church. It wasn't growing fast enough. The people weren't dedicated enough. He suspected that some of them used drugs or drank! And he preached angry, shouted sermons against this sin! To Marsha, some of those sermons sounded a lot like her father's angry outbursts.

It wasn't long before the pastoral committee met and decided to dismiss Cal. They said there wasn't much love in his preaching—it contained much more judgment, condemnation, and blame.

Cal was unable to obtain another pastorate, and he went into a serious depression. Finally, he got a job selling insurance. He seemed to work almost all the time. Marsha resented his work. She resented it as much as she had resented her father's using. When Cal was at home he was always either angry or depressed.

In fact, Cal seemed an awful lot like her father—but Cal didn't use drugs.

It wasn't until Sarah was fourteen that Marsha discovered the sexual abuse that her husband had been inflicting on their daughter. She was horrified to the point of considering homicide or suicide or both. She blamed herself, Cal's work, and the church that had fired him.

What never occurred to Marsha was that she had married a man with her father's personality, but who just didn't use drugs.

When Sarah was nineteen she met Ron. She felt comfortable around Ron. He seemed to have a lot of her father's personality except that he was less rigid and angry. In fact, he even smoked pot . . .

Note: This is just one of the many effects of addiction. Adults who grow up in addicted homes are affected, and so are their children and their children's children. For that reason, *it is essential for children of addicts to get help from a specialist who treats children of addicts.* If such help cannot be found while they are young, it is still crucial that they find it and work through their problems after they are adults.

Myth #8. Addiction can be cured.

Fact. An addict will always be an addict. An addict can be helped. He can reach the point of not using drugs (abstinence), but his body will always have an addictive potential. If he ever starts using again, he will be addicted again. His brain produces THIQ (see Myth #2) whenever he uses, and it always will. In addition, his brain already contains THIQ. If he starts using, in almost no time he will be experiencing severe addiction.

An addict or alcoholic who stops using can never use a mood-altering substance again. He can never learn to drink socially. He must remain drug-free for the rest of his life. Addiction can never be cured!

Many people who go through treatment think that they are cured. After a few months they deceive themselves into believing that they can drink socially. When they try, they soon discover that they are once again addicted.

Case Study: Brae had tried for years to beat alcohol and cocaine. She knew it was affecting her job, her relationship with her husband, Roy, the twins Bart and Brenda, and Casey. Brae had tried to quit by her own willpower over and over. She always failed.

But this time she had a plan! She had a month's sick leave built up at work, and she needed to have major surgery. She was scheduled to be in the hospital for a week. She talked her doctor into letting her stay two weeks. After that she intended to check herself into a chemical dependency program for two more weeks, telling her employer that she needed time to recuperate from surgery "at home."

After the surgery, the two weeks of treatment went well, but the staff at the treatment facility thought she needed an additional two weeks. She was out of time, however, and needed to get back to work.

Brae stayed straight for three years. She often announced that she had no problem with alcohol or cocaine. She had "beaten it." She was cured.

On her twenty-fifth wedding anniversary she decided that she could drink a glass of wine to celebrate. She did. In fact, she drank two.

She didn't drink again for three days. Within a month she was using more cocaine than she had used before she entered treatment. Bart and Brenda both dropped out of college, Bart to go into the military and Brenda to marry a man she barely knew, "to get away from home, if you want the truth." Casey is thinking of running away and probably would if he didn't feel that his dad needed him.

Myth #9. A drug addict is improving if he switches to a less powerful drug or starts drinking alcohol instead.

Fact. When an addict uses a different mood-altering substance, he is still practicing his addiction. All mood-altering chemicals are addictive. If alcohol were a new drug on the market today, it would be available only by prescription. *Alcohol meets all the requirements established for narcotics—extremely dangerous drugs.*

Addicts who switch from a powerful drug like heroin to a less powerful one like marijuana or alcohol soon return to using the more powerful drug. They also need more of it than they were using previously.

Case Study: Dan had been hooked on cocaine for ten years. He had done things to obtain cocaine that made him feel terrible about himself. His father owned the largest mobile-home lot in town, and Dan was his senior buyer. Whenever someone traded a mobile home to another dealer, Dan was paged to bid on it.

Each time he bought a mobile home, Dan added $300 to the receipt. His father never questioned him. He trusted Dan; honesty had always been an important value in their family. Each time Dan spent the money on cocaine.

Finally, Dan could stand it no more. He told his father about the cheating and that he was addicted. It was the first time Dan had ever seen his father cry. It was horrible!

But his father said he would help. He paid for Dan's treatment. Upon discharge from the hospital, Dan was referred to an outpatient counseling center. He met weekly with a therapist and seven other addicts. Talking to others made him anxious and nervous. He started smoking pot before meetings "to calm myself down. At least it isn't something as dangerous as heroin."

Buying mobile homes now also made Dan anxious. He wondered how many of the dealers knew about his addiction and his stealing from his father. Soon he was smoking pot or stopping off for a drink before going to bid on a trade.

One day he was driving past his drug dealer's house and stopped to say hello. By the time he left, he was loaded. The dealer had given him cocaine on credit. The next day Dan added $300 to the receipt he gave his father.

Danny Jr. knew about his father's "problem" and had been on the outs with him for several years because of it. Although Danny Jr.—known as D.J.—wanted to be close to his father, he found it very difficult, especially after he learned that Dan had cheated his grandfather, whom D.J. adored.

That night Dan came home to find his wife upset and worried; $20 had disappeared from her purse. Although D.J. was only fifteen, he was big for his age, and a few days earlier she had heard him on the telephone talking about a place where kids could buy beer "and if you look old enough they never bother to check your ID."

Myth #10. If I use drugs a few times nothing bad will happen.

Fact. That depends. If you have inherited a genetic tendency to produce THIQ, your first use will start the process described in Myth #2. Your first use may be exactly what sets the addictive process in motion. In addition, some drugs such as crack cocaine set the process in motion much faster than others. With crack, it is possible to become addicted in a single afternoon, or even with the very first usage.

Other drugs have a high "overdose potential"; that is, it is easy to kill yourself the first time you use the drug. In fact, every time you use cocaine it is possible to make a mistake that could be fatal. That is largely because of the effect the drug has on your heart and central nervous system. You could have a heart attack—yes, even at your age!—or a stroke, or go into a drug-induced coma.

Some people lack a blood enzyme necessary to break down drugs such as cocaine. Remember Lynn Bias? He could have been the best basketball player who ever lived.

Unfortunately, we'll never know. He died the first time he tried cocaine.

It is important to understand how drugs are distributed in this country. Drugs are passed from one supplier to another many times before they reach the users. Each supplier makes money by "cutting" the drug (adding ingredients to it).

Drugs have been cut with everything imaginable, including formaldehyde (which morticians use to embalm bodies), arsenic (a poison), and rat poison. You can never tell what is in a drug you buy on the street.

Occasionally, drugs go directly from the supplier to the user without being cut. That can be even more dangerous. In 1985, a shipment of 97 percent pure cocaine was seized on the turnpike between Tulsa and Oklahoma City. It was so strong that anyone who used it could have died instantly.

Case Study: Jack had never used cocaine, but he had heard that it gave one of the best "highs" possible. He knew that his wife, Kathy, had smoked cocaine and loved it. Nothing bad seemed to happen to her because of smoking cocaine.

Jack had been a football player in high school and college. Not yet forty, he still worked out and was in perfect physical condition. He kept in touch with guys he had played football with in college. Some of them were in the NFL now, and he knew some of them used. And nothing bad had happened to them. "So, why not?" he reasoned.

The last thing Jack remembered was the horrible crushing pain in his chest. He was dead on arrival at Memorial Hospital. He had suffered a massive heart attack.

Jackie, thirteen, and Richard, ten, were left without a

father and with a mother whose drug use was rapidly passing the "experimental" stage. Jackie thinks she can see what their future is going to be like, and it scares her half to death.

Myth #11. My dad can't be addicted. He only drinks beer.

Fact. There is approximately the same amount of alcohol in an eight-ounce can of beer, a glass of wine, a mixed drink, and a shot of whiskey. Some alcoholics only drink beer; others drink wine, beer, or whiskey depending on what is available.

Case Study: Jacob loved beer. He knew all about beer. He knew how it was made, how it was shipped, and at what temperature it should be served.

He never drank "hard liquor." After all, "Only alcoholics drink hard liquor." He was just "a hard-working, hard-playing, good ol' boy from Georgia." He'd been drinking beer all his life.

Jacob never stayed late at the bars; after all, he had a wife and family to look after. He drank a beer or two every night as soon as he got home. At least, that's the was it was for the first eight years. Then things began to change. Jacob was drinking more and more until he was putting away six to twelve cans of beer every evening and from a case to a case and a half on Saturday and again on Sunday.

His habits began to change. He stayed longer at the bars, and when he was home he watched television and drank beer late into the night.

Jacob also seemed angry most of the time he wasn't drinking. He had become rigid, controlling, and forgetful.

Things he forgot he blamed on his wife and sons. Sometimes he couldn't even remember how he had spent an evening. In short, Jacob was addicted to alcohol. Beer just happened to be his drug of choice.

Myth #12. People who are addicted simply lack willpower. They are weak or morally and spiritually sinful people.

Fact. Addiction has nothing to do with willpower. Addicts have lost control over a mood-altering substance or a mood-altering behavior. That does not happen because they are morally bad. It happens because they have inherited a genetic predisposition toward addiction.

Both medically and legally, alcoholism or addiction is classified as a disease. People who have it do not have a choice about it. They did not ask for it any more than someone would ask for cancer or multiple sclerosis.

It may be that the only mistake they made was taking that first drink, and the overwhelming majority of people have had at least one drink in their lives. After that, the addiction process was set in motion and couldn't be stopped simply by willpower or "wanting to."

It is important to remember that we should never hold an addict responsible for his addiction. But *we can and should hold an addict responsible for his recovery!* Once an addict knows that he is an addict, he should be held responsible for doing something about it.

Help is available.

Case Study: Heather's mom always seemed to be such a loving person. The kids liked to come to her house. It was a fun place to be. But little by little Heather's mom began to change. She was angry a lot of the time and yelled at Heather and other kids for things she once would have thought funny. She became moody, unpredictable, harshly critical of almost everything.

Heather was terribly upset by it all. She had no idea what was happening, or why. She began discouraging her friends from coming over, and she stayed away from home more and more herself. One day she realized how much her mother was drinking. She wondered if Mom was trying to drink her problems away—the fact that she was divorced, that money was tight, and things weren't going well on her job.

But those problems seemed to be getting better, not worse. Heather wondered what she could do. Trying to talk to her mother about it only drew anger. Heather felt helpess and scared.

In April, Aunt Mary came for a visit. She was Heather's favorite aunt, and for a while things seemed happy at home again. Then one day Heather came home to find her mother and Aunt Mary in the middle of a screaming argument. Mom was yelling, "Oh, why don't you mind your own business! This has nothing to do with you!"

Aunt Mary screamed back, "It is my business, and it has everything to do with me. You're the only sister I've got left. I love you, and you're letting alcohol destroy you and your whole family. Why, Heather told me she was ashamed of you and embarrassed to have friends come over any more. Don't you see what's happening? Didn't you see enough of it with Dad? The same thing is happening to you, and you're making Heather's life just like he made ours!"

Then Heather heard her mother start to cry and say softly, "Okay, I'll go. You're right, I just wouldn't admit it, even to myself. But who'll take care of the kids?"

Aunt Mary said, "I will," as her niece walked in.

"What's going on?" Heather asked.

Mom was mopping tears, and Aunt Mary said, "Your mom is sick, and we're going to get help for her. Don't worry, everything is going to be all right. You wait for the other kids to get home from school, and I'll be back in time to cook dinner."

Miraculously, everything *was* all right. Mom was in the hospital a little over a month, and while she was gone Aunt Mary was a pleasure for them all. Life was fun again.

When Mom came home, she was back the way she used to be. She was seeing a therapist to help her cope with the divorce and with the problems that come with alcoholism. A financial counselor was helping her get money matters straight.

Soon Heather was inviting her friends over again. One day one of them said, "Heather, you've got the neatest mom in the whole world." Heather looked up just in time to see tears in her mother's eyes.

She jumped up and hugged her mom. "We're like a fairy tale. Our story has a happy ending."

Myth #13. Sure, I'm addicted, but my habit will only hurt me. It's no one's business but mine. After all, it is my life."

Fact. Addiction is—unfortunately—everyone's business. It hurts everyone, even those who don't know the addicted person. Look at a few of the statistics. Drugs or alcohol are directly related to:

65% of all child-abuse cases
62% of all crimes
70% of all fatal falls
50% of all traffic deaths

67% of all suicide attempts
33% of all suicides
86% of all fire deaths
50% of all domestic battering
75% of all divorces
86% of all murders
43% of all nonaccident hospital admissions.

Chemical dependency is estimated to cost $78.6 billion a year in the United States alone. It isn't just the addicted person's business. *It's everybody's business.*

Myth #14. I know Dad's an addict, but I'm too young to become addicted.

Fact. It could take up to twenty years for a forty-year-old who starts using to develop a full-blown addiction. A twelve-year-old can do it in less than six months. A ten-year-old can do it in two months. The younger you start, the easier it is to get hooked, and the more severe the addiction. This doesn't mean that you will ever get old enough for drugs to be safe.

Case Study: Lucille was eleven and a half when she started using. By the time she was twelve she was using every day. Her grades had fallen, and she had became withdrawn and secretive. When her father put her in a hospital for what he thought was appendicitis, Lucille went into withdrawal, a sign of addiction of the most severe kind. In fact, Lucille almost died.

Case Study: Charles remembers his first drink very clearly. His father gave it to him when he was eight years old. "I can still remember how good it tasted, how great it made me feel. I'll tell you the truth, I think I was an alcoholic from that very first drink."

By the time he was eleven, Charles says, "My life revolved around being sure I could get something to drink. I became good at getting Dad's liquor and watering down what was left so he wouldn't see how much was gone. Even when he guessed I'd been drinking, he thought it was more funny than serious. Sometimes I waited outside liquor stores, and when I saw people put booze in their cars and then leave again, I'd try to steal the liquor. I usually could, too."

In high school Charles, in his own words, "drank enough booze every day to embalm a dinosaur." He had his driver's license for three months when he ran a stop sign, drunk, and killed two people. He is now serving time in a juvenile correctional facility.

Myth #15. OK, so I'm addicted. If I simply stop using everything will be fine.

Fact. There is no guarantee that everything will be fine. It depends on what, how much, and how long you've been using. There are four basic problems with the idea that things will return to normal if an addict quits using.

1. If the person was addicted to an inhalant, he will have some degree of brain damage. All drugs damage the brain, but inhalants do the most severe damage in the shortest time; that's an inescapable fact. When a user quits, his brain generally will not improve because damaged brain cells do not repair or replace themselves. Alcohol also causes severe damage that cannot be reversed, although to a lesser degree than inhalants.
2. If the person was addicted to psychedelics (drugs that cause hallucinations) such as PCP, LSD, mushrooms, or

peyote, he may have flashbacks (reexperiences of a drug trip) for some time or permanently.

3. All persons who are addicted will have problems with *alcoholic personality syndrome*. They tend to be rigid, controlling, angry, blaming, and they repress most other feelings. They have problems with intimacy with another person. They tend to have low self-image, to be defensive and manipulative. Only professional help, or in some cases self-help groups such as Alcoholics Anonymous or Narcotics Anonymous, can do much to change this.

4. Alcohol and drug addiction damage family relationships in such a way that only professional help can undo it. Children of addicted parents develop specific characteristics that last a lifetime and are passed on to their children (see Chapter 11). In addition, the spouse of an addict almost always suffers severe personality problems (see Chapter 7).

Myth #16. Mom can't be addicted. She only takes medicine her doctor gives her.

Fact. Most chemical dependency counselors believe that about twice as many people are addicted to prescription drugs as are addicted to illegal drugs.

Case Study: Rhonda was seriously injured in a traffic accident. She spent weeks in the Intensive Care Unit and was still in a wheelchair when discharged from the hospital. It would take months of therapy and muscle strengthening exercises before she would be able to walk again.

Rhonda was understandably angry at the way her life had been disrupted. During physical therapy, confronted yet again with her limitations and how far she had to go to recovery, she would often explode into anger and then into tears. Her doctor gave her medication to help with the pain and sleeping pills to help her rest at night. She also had medication to relieve the anxiety and depression brought on by the long ordeal.

After eight months Rhonda was walking with only a slight limp, although she still tired very easily. However, she continued to take all the medications she had needed during the worst part of her recovery. When her doctor recommended slowly cutting back on them, she become angry and fired him.

Rhonda then began to "shop doctors"—to go from doctor to doctor looking for several who would give her prescriptions for the drugs that her mind and body had become accustomed to and now craved. At the present time, she has sixteen doctors who prescribe medication for her. None of them knows about any of the others. She takes three different types of painkiller, one antianxiety drug, one antidepressant, and three types of sleeping pills. She uses a different pharmacy for each doctor.

Rhonda needs more and more medication because she is developing a higher level of tolerance as time goes by. She occasionally frightens her husband and her children by mixing her medications and alcohol, which they know can result in death.

Rhonda is addicted and could die of an overdose at any time.

SUMMARY

Addiction is the loss of control over mood-altering substances or behaviors.

Most addicts live in families and have jobs. People who

know them fairly well might never guess they have a problem.

Most addicts inherit a genetic potential for addiction. Others can still become addicted, but they must work at it. They usually are not bad people, nor do they lack willpower. They are able to stop drinking or using for short periods of time, but when they do use or drink they can never predict how much they will consume.

Addicts are of four basic types. Two are related to patterns of abuse: the daily addict and the binge addict. Two are related to genetic transmission: One is passed from father or mother to son or daughter; the other is passed only from father to son and is characterized by early and excessive drinking and extreme violence.

Addiction is a family disease; its effects can be seen for many generations. *Families that bear these addictive traits will need professional help even after generations have passed.*

Addiction can never be cured. An addict can never use a chemical without becoming more addicted. Severe problems can occur from just one use of an addictive chemical. Beer, wine, whiskey, amphetamines, narcotics, cocaine, psychedelics, inhalants, and barbiturates are all addictive.

Chemical dependency is a social problem because it affects everyone to some degree.

Anyone at any age can be addicted, but children and young people become addicted much faster than adults.

CHAPTER 3

The Drugs of Abuse

P eople have a natural curiosity about mood-altering drugs. Some of the questions most frequently asked are, "How many kinds of drugs are there?" "What are the proper and street names for these drugs?" "What are their medical uses?" "What do they look like?" Those questions are answered in this chapter.

STIMULANTS

Amphetamines

Amphetamines are medically known by the names Benzedrine, Desoxyn, Dexedrine, Biphetamine, dextroamphetamine, methamphetamine, and phenmetrazine.

The street names of these drugs include: dexies, uppers, pep pills, wake-ups, bennies, pushers, hearts, speed, meth, oranges, crystal, crank, bam, black beauties, glass of ice, white cross, black mollies, yellow jackets, bird-eggs, christmas trees, henis, black widows, and black birds.

The most common method of use is swallowing in pill

or capsule form. The drugs can also be used in powder form and snorted, or in liquid form injected into a vein (called "mainlining").

Medically, amphetamines were once commonly used for weight reduction, although that is rare now. A central nervous system stimulant, they are used in treatment of diseases such as the scleroses and dystrophies or the condition called narcolepsy, or sleeping sickness.

The symptoms of amphetamine use are excessive activity, sweating, dryness of the mouth, restlessness, increase in pulse and blood pressure, bad breath, mood swings, enlarged pupils, needle marks on arms or other areas where veins are easy to find, dizziness, wakefulness, talkativeness, irritability, irregular heartbeat, loss of touch with reality, and paranoia.

Use of speed over a long period of time, or a short period of very heavy use, can trigger outbursts of extreme, very dangerous, violence. An ambulance technician told of running a call for someone freaked out on amphetamines:

"He was in this small house, and we sat in the ambulance and watched him literally tear the place apart. These people have the strength of King Kong. We saw him grab a section of window, and when he pulled, half of the wall came out.

"When the cops got there and we went in after him, it took eight of us to subdue him. In the brawl his arm was broken, and that just barely got his attention."

In the book *Fatal Vision*, author Joe McGuinness writes about Jeff MacDonald, a doctor and a captain in the Green Berets. He speculates that MacDonald might have "flipped out" and gone on the rampage that ended in the murder of his pregnant wife and two small daughters after taking amphetamines to lose weight.

Other hazards of abuse of speed include brain damage, convulsions, hallucinations, paranoia, and death from overdose.

Amphetamines come in a wide variety of forms: pills, capsules, powder, liquid, or crystalline. Both crystal and the new designer drug, ice, come in crystalline form.

Cocaine

Cocaine is medically known by that name: cocaine.

The street names include coke, Bernie, toot, girl, C, white lady, snow, cecil, crack, nose candy, and blow. Crack, the designer form of cocaine, is an extremely fast-cycling stimulant to which persons can become addicted in one afternoon.

The most common method of use is by snorting (inhaling). It may also be swallowed, injected, or free-based (combined with another chemical and smoked).

Medically cocaine has a history of use as an anesthetic. It has no other known medical use.

The symptoms of use include excessive excitability, restlessness, nervousness, enlarged pupils, nausea, violent behavior, anxiety, paranoia, increased urination, loose stools, elevated blood pressure, feelings of well-being followed by depression, intense periods of euphoria, and increased pulse rate.

The hazards of abuse are damage to nasal passages, cardiovascular difficulties, and death from overdose. Recently, researchers have discovered that some persons lack a blood enzyme that breaks down cocaine. In these persons one experimental dose can prove fatal.

Like the amphetamines, cocaine use can set off rampages of extreme violence combined with almost super-human strength.

Evidences of cocaine use include glass pipes, razor blades, white crystalline powder, syringes, and needle marks on the arms or other places where veins are easily accessible.

DEPRESSANTS

Tranquilizers

Medically, tranquilizers are known as phenobarbital, secobarbital, Nembutal, amobarbital, Seconal, Amytal, Butizone, Noctec, Sopor, Luminal, Dramamine, Benadryl, Lompazine, Mellaril, Thorazine, Phenergan, Nartec, Equanil, Miltown, Nolander, Doriden, Ativan, Xanax, Restoril, Halcion, Bonex, Valium, Dalmane, Serax, Quaalude, Centrax, Placidyl, Librium, methaqualone, and Tranxene.

The street names of these drugs are downers, goof balls, yellow jackets, barbs, red devils, blue devils, reds, tranks, blues, yellows, peanuts, numby dolls, Mickey Finns, jelly beans, sopos, goofers, peaches, ludes, 714s, muscle relaxants, and sleeping pills.

The most common methods of use are swallowing pills or capsules, or, in liquid form, injecting into a vein.

The medical usage is as a sedative in muscle spasms and nervousness and anxiety.

The symptoms of use are confusion, slurred speech, impaired judgment, disorientation, intoxicated behavior, depressed breathing and heartbeat, staggering gait, depressed blood pressure, loss of appetite, inappropriate feelings of well-being, drowsiness, and poor coordination.

The hazards of abuse are addiction with severe withdrawal symptoms, depressed cardiovascular functioning, and death from overdose.

Tranquilizers come in blue, red, yellow, and red/blue capsules, white or pale yellow powder, and liquid form. Evidences of usage include needle marks on skin, syringes, various containers with a powder or powder residue in them, or the finding of the tablets themselves.

Narcotics

Medically these drugs are known as Darvon, Percodan, codeine, heroin, methadone, morphine, Empirin, Tylenol with codeine, and Darvocet.

The street names of these drugs are: horse, H, smack, boy, junk, dreamer, school boy, stuff, nord, sugar, tea, dolls, dolly, black tar, china white, joy powder, dope seat, harry morph, and big M.

The most common methods of use are swallowing in pill form and injecting into the arm or other place where the veins are available. Some forms may be used rectally.

Medical usages include pain relief and, in the case of methadone, withdrawal from other narcotics.

The symptoms of use are euphoria, drowsiness, slurred speech, lethargy, needle marks, constipation, narrowed pupils, flushed skin (face, neck, and chest), respiratory depression, nausea, chills and sweating, cramps, watery eyes, tremors, cold skin, and moist skin.

The hazards of abuse are depressed cardiovascular functioning, coma, and death from overdose.

Narcotics come in pill or liquid form. Other signs of use are needles, syringes, and spoons.

Alcohol

More people are addicted to alcohol than to any other chemical in the world. It is also the most fatal addictive substance in the world. Some two hundred thousand alcohol-related deaths occur each year in the United States, compared to six hundred deaths related to cocaine.

The appropriate medical name of this drug is ethyl alcohol.

Among the street names are: beer, wine, whiskey, rye, brandy, scotch, booze, drink, shot, hooch, juice, brew, taste, mountain dew, firewater, highball, cocktail, liquor, moonshine, white lightning.

The method of use is drinking in liquid form.

The symptoms of use are staggering gait, impaired judgment, poor muscle coordination, slurred speech, relaxed inhibitions, poor depth perception, slow reflexes, intoxication, nausea, vomiting, blackouts (drug-induced amnesia), slowed breathing, and decreased sexual performance.

The hazards of use include liver disease, severe withdrawal symptoms (including delirium tremens, shakes, esophageal hemorrhage, elevated blood pressure, and auditory/visual hallucinations), heart failure, respiratory failure, blackouts, progressive memory loss, brain damage, and violent behavior.

The evidence of use is usually beer bottles (or cans), alcohol and wine bottles, and hangovers (bloodshot eyes, headache, upset stomach, shakes, and impaired thinking).

Stimulant or Depressant

This class of drug represents a special case. It is the only drug that may act as either a stimulant or a depressant, depending upon the emotional state of the user. The appropriate medical name is Dexamyl.

The street names of the drug are greenies and copilots.

The medical uses of this drug are for hyperactivity and weight loss.

The symptoms of use may be either excitability or depression.

This drug comes in pill form. It is green in color.

HALLUCINOGENS

Marijuana

The appropriate medical name of this drug is Cannabis.

The street names for it are pot, weed, Acapulco Gold, reefer, Mary Jane, Colombian, Texas tea, grass, Mary J, Wanna, joint, rope, roach, Jamaican, and Maui Wowie.

The methods of use are smoking in cigarettes, pipes, or bongs and ingesting in food (especially brownies.)

Medically marijuana is sometimes used in the treatment of glaucoma and—because it powerfully stimulates the appetite—to help cancer patients gain weight. It was once used to treat asthma.

The symptoms of use are a sweet, burnt odor, loss of interest or loss of motivation, weight gain, red or bloodshot eyes, chronic cough, chest pain, impaired concentration/coordination, lethargy, increased appetite, and unkempt appearance.

The hazards of abuse are mood swings, possible damage to the reproductive system, lung disease, emotional retardation, panic reaction, impaired memory, brain damage, and interference with learning. It often leads to addiction to other more powerful drugs.

Evidences of use are marijuana seeds, roaches (the butts of marijuana cigarettes), a bong (a jar with a long hose and mouthpiece for smoking), pipes, cigarette papers, marijuana plant stems, plastic bag with marijuana seeds and/or plant stems, roach clips, and burn holes in shirts, blouses, or other clothing.

A form of marijuana is hashish, which is five to ten times stronger than marijuana. It is known by the street names charas, ganja, bhang, Sinsemilla-hash, hash, Lebanese blonde, cheese, or hash oil.

A form called red oil of cannabis is up to forty-five times stronger than the typical marijuana cigarette.

Hashish is sometimes ground into a light brown powder and mixed into drinks or candies, or laced into marijuana cigarettes to increase their potency.

PCP

The appropriate medical names for this drug are phencyclidine and Sernyl. It was originally developed as an animal tranquilizer.

The street names for the drug are angel dust, super grass, hog, killer weed, and peace pill.

The most common method of using PCP is smoking. It is usually laced into marijuana cigarettes. It can also be snorted or swallowed.

The symptoms of use include blurred vision, agitation, confusion, uncoordination, slurred speech, panic, nausea, and a mixing of the senses (such as being able to hear colors or smell music. This is not to be confused with the "sixth sense" that some people have naturally, which is a blending of the senses called *synesthesia*).

The hazards of use include extreme anxiety or depression or both, impaired memory, chronic perceptual difficulties, accident proneness, extreme aggressive tendencies that sometimes result in homicide, and death from overdose.

The drug may be found in capsules, tablets, or powder.

LSD

The appropriate medical name of this drug is lysergic acid diethylamide.

The street names for it are acid, cubes, pearly gates, wedding bells, zen, business man's trip, purple haze, mirodot, window pane, orange sunshine, vitamin A, blotter, and orange barrels.

The most common method of use is ingestion of a drop placed on a sugar cube. It can also be injected, swallowed in tablets, or skin-popped (held against the skin until absorbed).

There is no known medical use for this drug.

The symptoms of use include dilated pupils, hallucinations, mood swings, illusions, loss of touch with reality, depression, increased pulse rate, confusion, euphoria, trancelike states, tremors, seeing faces in objects, seeing things as larger or smaller than they are, seeing people with halos, intensification of colors, flashes of color, and afterimages of objects.

The hazards of use include loss of touch with reality that is sometimes permanent, flashbacks, emotional breakdown, and permanent brain damage.

Evidences of use include discovery of the chemical in pill, liquid, or blotter-square form. It may also be found absorbed in sugar cubes or cartoon character tattoos.

Mescaline

The medical name of this drug is peyote.

The street names are peyote, mesc, cactus buttons, and Yanqui adventure.

The most common method of use is eating in its natural form. It can also be found in powder form.

The symptoms of use are hallucinations, mood swings, dilated pupils, loss of touch with reality, trancelike state, euphoria, increased pulse rate, and confusion.

The hazards of use are emotional breakdown and brain damage.

The strongest evidence of mescaline usage, besides the above symptoms, is physical evidence of cactus buttons.

Psilocybin

The medical name is psilocybin.

The street names of the drug are magic mushroom, red tops, schrooms, toadstools, and Alice in Wonderland.

The most common form of use is eating in its natural form.

Psilocybin has no known medical uses.

The symptoms of use are mood swings, hallucinations, illusions, dilated pupils, and loss of touch with reality.

The hazards of use include emotional breakdown that may be permanent and brain damage.

The evidence of use, other than the above symptoms, is discovery of the fungus itself.

Organic Solvents

Inhalants are found in many forms, including aerosol products such as spray paint and hair spray, and volatile solvents such as gasoline, antifreeze, lighter fluid, transmission fluid, airplane glue, nail polish remover, typewriter correction fluid, vegetable cooking sprays, and paint thinner.

Among street names for these products are bolt snapper, whippits, laughing gas, Pam, glue, rush, locker room, and White-Out.

Methods of use of aerosol products are inhaling the spray directly from the can or spraying its contents into a paper bag and then inhaling. Volatile solvents are inhaled directly from the container; poured into a beer or soda pop can and inhaled, or poured into a cloth that is placed over the user's nose and mouth and inhaled ("huffing").

The symptoms of use are impaired coordination, judgment, vision, and memory; dizziness, headache, loss of bowel or bladder control, fatigue, and nausea.

The hazards of use are irrevocable liver, brain, and blood damage.

Evidences of use include rags, cans, dried glue on face, and odor of chemicals on breath.

COMMONLY ASKED QUESTIONS

Question: I think my mother uses more than one drug. Could she be addicted to both of them?

Answer: Yes. In fact, about half of all addicts are addicted to more than one drug. It is called *polyaddiction*.

Question: I know that some addicts have a favorite drug. When they can't get that, will they use a similar acting drug?

Answer: Yes, the favorite drug is referred to as the *drug of choice*. When that drug is unavailable, they will use one that is similar. For instance, a person who uses crystal will use crack when crystal is unavailable.

Question: My dad seems to use two very different kinds of drugs. Could he be addicted to drugs that are different or even opposite to each other?

Answer: Yes. Dual addiction is quite common.
An example is the person who uses de-
pressants to control anxiety and stimulants
to control the depression. One gets him
up, the other gets him down.

Why Your Parent Is So "Moody"

Every addict experiences certain drug-induced changes in mood. These mood swings follow a predictable pattern. However, each addict behaves differently depending on the drug or combination of drugs that he uses. The basic addictive cycle goes like this:

1. Pain-relieving use of a chemical or performance of a pain-relieving act.
2. Guilt or loss of self-esteem.
3. Experience of emotional pain, which could be depression, anxiety, or intense boredom.
4. Obsessive thinking about, using, or acting out.
5. Use of a pain-relieving chemical or performance of a pain-relieving act.

It looks like this:

An addict behaves differently depending on where he is in the addictive cycle. That can be very confusing to friends and family. Each of the stages in the addictive cycle impacts everyone who is involved with the user.

The Downer Cycle

People who abuse downers (barbiturates, alcohol, narcotics, etc.) follow this same pattern, but they are in a very distinct kind of emotional pain when they are not using. They feel anxious. For them, the addictive cycle looks like this:

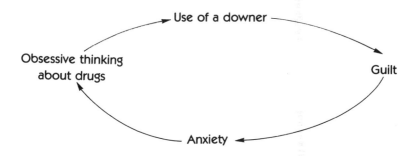

Case Study: Martin's father was an addict. Martin was never quite sure how he would react to anything. But at times he was very generous. He bought his son gifts, gave him spending money, took him places, even took his friends to the movies.

Martin didn't realize that at these times his father was recovering from using drugs and feeling guilty about it.

At other times asking for a couple of dollars for something he needed for school would make Dad lash out angrily. These reactions were tied to anxiety.

At still other times Dad would be remote, distant, not quite seeming to see or hear Martin. At those times Dad had drugs on his mind, and shortly afterward he would disappear for a couple of days. When he came home, he would give Martin anything he wanted and some things he didn't even ask for.

Martin, like most children of addicts, lived in a world of emotional Russian roulette.

The Upper Cycle

The primary difference between addiction to uppers (speed, crystal, crank, cocaine, crack) and downers is that the downer addict is anxious when he isn't using whereas the upper addict is depressed when he isn't using. The behavior of the upper user is very confusing to friends and family. The upper cycle looks like this:

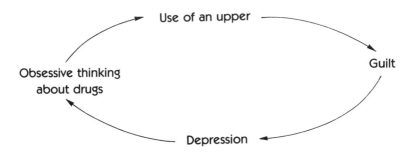

Case Study: Kelly's mother was a speed freak, addicted to crank. Kelly knew she used drugs but didn't understand why she was so mean sometimes. When she was using she talked nonstop and was always moving. "Being around her makes you feel sandpapered!" Kelly told a friend. It made her want to grab her mother and scream at her just to hold still and be quiet!

After her mom stopped using she would cry and say how sorry she was and that she was a terrible mother.

Kelly would try to console her, but it never seemed to work; no matter what she did, Mom would get worse and worse. She would be quiet and withdrawn, often locking herself in the bedroom and coming out only long enough to eat the meals Kelly cooked.

Then would begin the telephone calls to her dealer and other drug-using friends, the efforts to get together enough money for more crank. Kelly dreaded those times. When Mom reached that point she was hostile and sarcastic, sometimes slapping or punching Kelly without reason or justification. During those times Kelly was very much afraid of her.

The Upper/Downer Cycle

This cycle can be extremely confusing to the child of an addict. The upper/downer cycle happens when a person is dually addicted, using one chemical to get up and another to get down. The cycle looks like this:

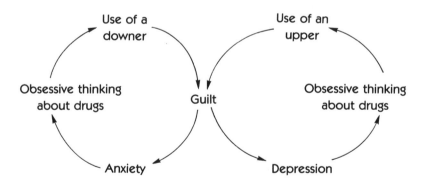

As can be seen from the diagram, the person addicted to uppers and downers is predictably unpredictable. His family and friends can never be certain where he is on the cycle. They can never be certain whether guilt will be followed by use of an upper or a downer, or whether the person will be depressed or anxious later.

What makes it even more confusing is that sometimes when addicts are down (after using a downer) they seem happy, and at other times when they are down (when they are depressed) they are miserable. The same is true for those times when they are up. Sometimes (after using uppers) they are frenetic, always moving, bionic-mouthed talkers, and sometimes (coming up after using a downer) they are extremely anxious and angry. No one has any idea what to expect.

Case Study: Charlotte's mother was addicted to crystal and Quaaludes. She felt certain she needed both drugs just to survive, to get through each day. One day Charlotte found her mother curled up and sobbing in a corner of the living room. Charlotte sat down with her, tried to cheer her up, told her everything was going to be fine, but Mom hardly seemed to hear her. She seemed remote, unreachable.

A week later Charlotte found her mother in the same corner, seeming depressed but also at peace. She was singing, over and over, an old song called "Mellow Yellow."

The next day Mom was angry and agitated. When Charlotte tried to understand what was going on, Mom slapped her viciously and began screaming at her.

But two days later Mom wanted to talk. In fact, she sat in Charlotte's room talking until 4 a.m., even though Charlotte had two tests the next day at school. Mom wasn't making a lot of sense, but she was talking!

To her boyfriend, Charlotte described her life at home as "a roller coaster through hell."

The Hallucinogen Cycle

People who use hallucinogens (PCP, LSD, peyote, mushroom) are a special case. Their cycle has some very strange components. That is especially true if the person actually uses in the presence of family members because of the unreal things a hallucinogen causes the user to see, hear, and smell.

It is not unusual for a user to think that he or she can fly, to carry on a conversation with a person who is dead, or to believe snakes have invaded the house.

One use may cause pleasant delusions such as having sex or seeing beautiful colors; the next use may cause fearful delusions such as being attacked by a monster or seeing blood everywhere.

One of the scariest things about these drugs is that a flashback can happen at any time. A flashback is a reexperience of a drug trip, good or bad, when the addict is not using. It can be very dangerous.

Imagine that a parent has a flashback while driving a car on a busy interstate highway. All of a sudden he is seeing rivers of beautiful colors. His children can't understand what is happening. All they know is that the car is out of control and Dad seems very happy.

The hallucinogen cycle looks like this:

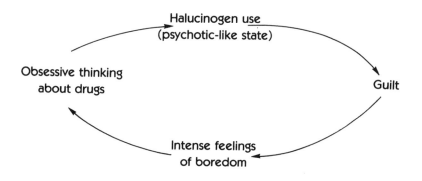

Because of the powerful action of hallucinogens on the brain, users are completely unpredictable. That is especially true during flashbacks. The content of a flashback experience is also unpredictable.

Case Study: Ginny and her family were finally going on vacation. Everybody was happy and excited in the van, with Mom driving down Interstate 10. In less than two hours they would be at Grandmother's house.

Dad seemed to be half asleep when all of a sudden he began lashing out and screaming, "Leave me alone! Leave me alone!" although no one had touched him or even spoken to him. Before anyone could stop him, he opened the door and jumped out of the van.

By the time Mom stopped and everybody ran back to find Dad, several vehicles had run over him. An autopsy found nothing to explain what had happened. But after the funeral Dad's brother revealed that he had been a heavy user of LSD in college, fifteen years ago.

LIVING WITH AN ADDICTED PARENT

As mentioned earlier, most addicts lead lives that are outwardly fairly normal. People who know them often have no idea that they have a problem.

But for family members, that problem dominates their lives.

The word most used by the children of addicts to describe their lives is uncertainty. They never know from one minute to the next how Mom is going to act, what Dad is going to do.

When they get up in the morning, will Dad smile and say "Good morning"? Or will he backhand them because they smile and say "Good morning"? When they come home from school, will Mom be in the kitchen baking cookies, or will she be passed out on the living room floor? Will they have money to go to the game as promised, or will it all have been spent on crack? Will Dad come home tonight, or will they get a call that he is in jail, or the hospital, or the morgue?

Will they have a home to come home to much longer? Dad has been having job problems because of his drinking, and if he is fired . . .

Cory, fifteen, puts it very well. "You just never have any idea what to expect. You learn not to get your hopes up for anything. You also learn never to trust what they say, or any promises they make. You take it all with, 'Yeah, I'll believe it when I see it, okay?'"

In most families a lot of effort is put into concealment, denial, "putting up a front," so that outsiders will not know that anything is wrong.

There is often a great deal of isolation. Children are not encouraged to have friends come over—they might see Dad crocked or realize that the smoke in the kitchen where Mom is didn't come from burned biscuits. Often children are restricted in their attempts to form other friendships or have a social life outside the home, lest they "let something slip."

Money is often a real problem, even though the family may appear to be affluent.

As the daughter of one addict puts it, "Nobody can understand why I don't have money for a lot of things at school and don't have nice clothes when we live in an expensive house and Dad's an executive with his company. They don't know how much money goes up his and Mom's nose. I heard her tell him once that they'd spent almost $1,000 for cocaine in *one week*! Yet they couldn't come up with enough money for me to have a pep squad uniform. People look shocked when I say I hate my parents, but I do. I really do!"

Physical or sexual abuse or both are much more likely to happen to children. Even though a parent may have been violent only once or twice, or perhaps never has been violent, family members usually feel that the potential is always there. The son of one alcoholic, who had been hit only twice while his father was drunk, said, "I know he could always lose control again. It's like walking on eggs, the way you feel you have to act around him."

If other parents knew about your parent's addiction, they might hold it against *you*, for example not allowing a son or daughter to go out with you or go to your house.

Family members are put into roles. Almost no one is allowed to be himself or herself, to be the kind of person he or she would be in a family that did not have a problem.

Sometimes the roles in the family are reversed, with you being given, or taking on, the job of taking care of and being responsible for a parent, instead of the other way around.

Almost universally, say the children of addicted parents, it robs you of your childhood. You will not have childhood memories like other people. Your childhood has been lost trying to cope with a parent's addiction.

CHAPTER 5

Why Your Parent

Doesn't Just Stop

F or centuries it was thought that addiction came about because of a person's inborn sinful nature. Addicts were seen as having a basic problem with willpower. In other words, they were evil and could not control their evil impulses.

Today, however, that has changed. In 1956 the American Medical Association referred to addiction and alcoholism as a disease, and it is now so classified both medically and legally.

Social workers, psychologists, marriage and family therapists, and drug and alcohol counselors today refer to and treat addiction as a disease.

The term *disease* has been defined in several ways:

1. A pathological syndrome (unhealthy condition) having a group or set of concurrent symptoms (several symptoms at the same time).
2. An abnormal condition of an organ, or part,

especially as a result of infection, inherent weakness, or environmental stress, that impairs normal functioning.

3. A pathological state that has a known etiology (cause), a predictable course, and a definite outcome.

It makes little difference which of these definitions you use. It is clear that alcohol or drug addiction fits all of them.

We know that drug addiction is "a pathological syndrome having a set of concurrent symptoms." We also know that it is "an abnormal condition as a result of inherent weakness that impairs normal functioning."

This chapter is largely conerned with describing the "known etiology, predictable course, and definite outcome" mentioned in definition three.

A Known Etiology

Etiology means cause. The cause was described in Chapter 1. Persons become addicted because they have inherited a genetic predisposition to create THIQ in their brain.

A Predictable Course

That means that the addiction will follow a certain pattern in all persons. This course has three definite stages: chemical (early), behavioral (middle), and chronic (late).

Early Stage—Chemical

1. First sign: increased tolerance of alcohol or drugs.
2. Has blackouts (not everyone has them).

3. Sneaks drinks or drugs.
4. Is preoccupied with drinking or drugs.
5. Uses alcohol or drugs to relieve anxiety.
6. Avoids references to addiction.
7. Is uncomfortable in situations without drugs or alcohol.
8. Loses control.
9. Needs to use before or after social occasions.

Middle Stage—Behavioral

10. Is dishonest about use of alcohol or drugs.
11. Invents alibis.
12. Tries to control use of alcohol or drugs.
13. Reproves self.
14. Drinks or uses drugs alone or secretly.
15. First drink or drug use becomes urgent.
16. Shows extravagance.
17. Readily shows jealousy and is sometimes unreasonable.
18. Experiences decrease in sexual capacity.
19. Exhibits aggression.
20. Neglects eating.
21. From time to time attempts to stop using.
22. Feels remorse.
23. Incurs disapproval of family and associates.
24. Rationalizes and excuses use of alcohol or drugs.
25. Changes pattern of use.
26. Lets social life decay.
27. Has family difficulties.
28. Has problems on job.
29. Seeks help.
30. Accumulates a list of resentments.
31. Attempts a solution by moving.

32. Maintains and protects supply.
33. Has episodes of chain drinking or using.
34. Undergoes physical and psychological changes.

Late Stage—Chronic

35. Engages in early-morning use of alcohol or drugs.
36. Undergoes moral deterioration.
37. Has chronic health problems.
38. Experiences persistent and unyielding grief.
39. Undergoes hospitalization.
40. Lets nuclear family break down.
41. Overworks excuses.
42. Engages in illogical thinking.
43. Goes on longer binges.
44. Cannot work.
45. Experiences intense jealousies.
46. Uses with increasingly lower social classes.
47. Has impaired thinking.
48. Has decreased tolerance.
49. Suffers undefinable fears.
50. Has tremors and shakes.
51. Develops psychomotor inhibitions (physical impairment of, for example, hand-eye coordination).
52. Resorts to religious consumption (praying to keep a drink down).
53. Death.

Note: No one addict has all symptoms.

A Definite Outcome

Unfortunately, all drug addiction that is allowed to run its course unchecked is fatal.

All untreated drug addicts and alcoholics die pre-
maturely from physical illness, suicide, or accident—all
associated with their addiction. The statistics speak for
themselves. Alcohol or drugs are involved in:

45% of all nonaccident hospital admissions
50% of all fatal traffic accidents
33% of all suicides
86% of all fire fatalities
65% of all drownings
70% of all fatal falls.

CHAPTER ◇ 6

What's Happening
to Your Parent's
Personality

People who are addicted tend to use very specific defense mechanisms to deal with the emotional pain of being addicted. Those defenses are: denial, projection, minimization, displacement, blaming, expression of anger, repression of feelings, blackouts with confabulation, and rigidity.

Denial

Denial is defined as the psychological process of not knowing the extent of one's own addiction. Those who are addicted to a mood-altering chemical do not know how much of the chemical they use or how frequently they use it.

Case Study: Rose's mother was an alcoholic. She was rarely at home when Rose came in from school. This afternoon was no different. As soon as she entered the house Rose noticed the beer cans on the coffee table, the couch, and the floor. She picked them up and took them to the trash can in the kitchen.

The next afternoon Rose went with her mother to keep an appointment with the doctor, who seemed very concerned about her.

He asked a question that Rose couldn't quite hear, but her mother's answer was clear: "Yes, I drink a beer now and then."

The doctor asked "How many do you drink?"

"Never more than two or three."

Rose stared in astonishment. "But Mom, yesterday you drank at least twenty before you went out. I know—I put the cans in the trash!"

Now it was her mother's turn to stare. "Whatever are you talking about, honey? I don't drink twenty cans of beer a year!"

Projection

Projection is defined as subconsciously transferring emotional pain to another person. When projection is used to deal with pain, the addict does not experience his own pain. He believes that it belongs to someone else.

Case Study: Carol's father came home from work early one day. Carol was surprised, because he was usually late, stopping off at bars on the way home.

She asked, "What are you doing home so early?"

"I got laid off," her father replied calmly.

"Oh, Dad, how awful! Are you okay? I mean, is everything all right?"

"It's okay. And I'm all right. But you should have seen how upset my secretary was! And poor Mr. Johnson, I thought he was going to start crying when he told me he had to let me go!"

Minimization

Minimization is the psychological defense of grossly underrating the importance of certain events.

Case Study: Stanley and Bruno were playing on the grounds at recess when they saw a police car pull up in front of the school. Bruno said, "Wow! Stan, that's your dad in that cop car. What's going on?"

Wide-eyed, Stanley said, "I don't know, but it looks like Mom's there and they're looking for me." Both boys began to run.

"Dad, what's going on? Is something wrong?"

"I guess so. That mother of yours, always smoking in bed! Now she's burned the house down!"

Stanley knew that Mom also drank in bed and that his parents were always fighting about it. Now he began to cry. "Dad, that's awful! Where will we live?"

"Look, it's no big deal," his mother said, getting unsteadily out of the police car. "We needed a new house anyway."

Stanley could tell that his father was very upset, but his mother just staggered a little as she walked up to the fence. "What's all the fuss about, anyway?"

Displacement

Displacement is taking out your anger on someone other than the person with whom you are angry.

Case Study: Darrel's father had had a bad afternoon at work. At lunch time he had slipped away to smoke a couple of marijuana cigarettes, and during the afternoon he was more often chatting with coworkers or blundering around running into things than really doing his job. Just before quitting time he got a royal chewing-out from the foreman and was told that unless his job performance improved he would be fired.

He was furious with the foreman but didn't dare do anything but stand there and say, "Yes, sir," "No, sir." But the minute he got home that evening he began to scream at Darrel for having things scattered on the dining room table (Darrel was doing his homework), and at his wife because dinner wasn't ready (he had said he would take them out for pizza that night).

He didn't dare hit back at the foreman, but his son and his wife were "safe" targets for his temper.

The children of addicts are the subjects of a lot of displaced anger.

Blaming

Blaming is the psychological defense of holding someone else responsible for one's own behavior.

Case study: Gretchen's mother was stoned out of her mind when she came in that evening, and Dad was furious. He bellowed, "You've blown your paycheck on cocaine again, damn you! You're nothing but a coke-head, and that's all you'll ever be! My mother was right about you! You'll never amount to anything and you'll never quit!"

Her mother began to scream back, "Oh, really! You want to know why I need to use coke? Look in the mirror, you wimp! It's all your fault. You and that damned daughter of yours. I wouldn't need it if it weren't for the two of you, hanging on me, wanting this and that . . . It's not *my* fault. I'm a victim of circumstances."

Sure.

Repression of Feelings

This psychological defense is self-explanatory. Addicts operate somewhat like robots. They experience few emotions, because they typically repress their feelings.

Case Study: Celia's father was coming down from using speed, and to her he seemed pretty depressed. She wasn't sure whether it was because of the drugs or because his mother had just passed away and they had always been close. Celia decided to try to comfort him. He was sitting on the couch, just staring at the wall, and he seemed so alone.

She sat down beside him and said, "I love you, Dad, and I'm so sorry about Grandmother. I bet you miss her a lot."

"Not really," her father said, remotely. "She never really knew me. I guess she was all right."

Then he got up and left. Somehow Celia knew he was going after more speed.

Expression of Anger

Anger is usually the only feeling that is expressed freely by an addicted person.

Case Study: Adam's father is a binge alcoholic. He isn't always drunk, but he is always angry. Adam can barely remember a normal conversation with him. Most attempts to talk end up with Dad yelling at the top of his lungs. Most of the time Adam just avoids his father when that is possible.

Most of the family avoids him, too, so Dad has taken his anger outside and spends a lot of time picking fights with the neighbors. He threatened to shoot a neighbor's dog that got out and was playing on his lawn. When the fat woman across the street works in her front yard, he yells insults. He called the police because smoke from the next-door neighbor's grill was coming into his backyard. Once Adam heard the neighbors on each side joking about going halves on a hit man.

Adam used to get along well with the people in the neighborhood, but now everyone is so disgusted with his father that they are beginning to act as if they don't want *him* around.

Blackouts with Confabulation

A blackout is a period of amnesia, of being unable to remember the events of a certain period of time. Blackouts occur because of excessive use of mood-altering chemicals. They can occur at any time, even when the addict is sober or not on drugs.

Confabulation is a psychological defense against the effects of a blackout. It is filling in the memory gaps with a made-up sequence of events. In other words, the addict invents a version of what happened during the blackout. When that occurs it is very difficult to convince the addict that his version is not the truth.

Case Study: Melissa's dad was in a great mood. She enjoyed it so much when he was like this. They were watching a television special together, and he was funnier than anything on the screen. She laughed until she cried and her sides hurt. Then her mother came home from a meeting.

"How'd the evening go?" she asked.

Melissa's father replied, "Okay, I guess. I watched TV for a while, and Melissa was upstairs in her room."

Astonished, Melissa stared at him and said, "But, Dad, I was right here with you, watching TV, too!"

"Don't be ridiculous," her father snapped. "I've hardly seen you this evening, and after I stayed here especially to watch TV with you. You act as if everything else comes before the family. See if I make another effort to spend time with you!" and he slammed the door as he left the room.

"Mom, Mom!" Melissa cried, "I was right here!"

Melissa's mother glared at her. "You could give some time to your dad. All you ever think about is yourself."

Melissa went slowly up to her room, wondering if she were going insane.

Rigidity

Rigidity is defined as disallowing new ways of thinking. The addicted person rejects new ideas, new ways of doing or thinking about anything.

Case Study: Paul's father was addicted to marijuana and, Paul thought, also used other drugs from time to time. He was a plumber whose job it was to install gas lines between butane tanks and houses. One summer Paul agreed to work with his father. Although Dad would not admit it, Paul could see that he was falling farther and farther behind in his work, and his boss was becoming more and more impatient with him. Recently he had threatened to fire him. Paul was determined to help—that was something all the family were afraid might happen.

When they arrived at the job site early in the morning Paul grabbed a pick and shovel and shouted, "I'll dig this one, you dig that one." He finished his ditch in about twenty minutes and ran back to where his father was toiling away. "I'm through," he said.

His father scowled and snapped, "Bull! You couldn't possibly be through."

Then Paul looked at the ditch his father was digging. It was only about a fourth done, but it had *straight* sides and a *flat* bottom, and Paul knew that his father wasn't going to like his ditch.

"Let's see," his dad said, and walked to where Paul had been working. Sure enough, he didn't like it. "That's not how you dig a ditch! A ditch has *straight* sides and a flat bottom. Get back in there and get to work!"

"But Dad," Paul protested, "we're just going to lay a gas line in it and cover it up again, aren't we? What does it matter what the thing *looks* like?"

His father ignored that and kept screaming at him for not knowing how to dig a ditch and being lazy on top of that. Paul shrugged and went back to work, and eventually his ditch had straight sides and a flat bottom. But during lunch he noticed that another man on the crew, a guy named John, had dug a ditch just like Paul's, and the boss walked by and looked approving.

Two days later Paul's father was fired. Paul heard him complaining to his mother, "He has given John more hours, and John doesn't even know how to dig a ditch, not to mention lay pipe."

Paul's father's thinking was so locked into digging a ditch the way *he* thought it should be that he didn't even notice that his work was too slow and he wasted a lot of time. When the boss tried to point that out to him, he argued about it.

"WHAT CAN *I* DO ABOUT A PARENT'S ADDICTION/ALCOHOLISM?"

Unfortunately, probably not very much.

You may have heard, and it is certainly true, that addicts can change only when *they* want to change. Almost never can they be bullied, reasoned with, shamed, made to feel guilty, or emotionally blackmailed into trying to break free of addiction.

Unhappily, family members seldom realize that, or realize it in time to save themselves a lot of anguish.

A child's efforts to get a parent to stop drinking or using can run a wide range: "Don't you love us enough to stop hurting us like this?" "Dad, you could quit, if you wanted to. People quit all the time. Please do it for us!" "You don't care about us! Geting high on coke is all in this world that matters to you!" "Driving drunk like that, you are going to have a wreck and kill someone. How will you feel then?" "Mom, if you didn't love us enough to take care of us like a real mother, why did you have us in the first place?" "Dad, did you know Bob has started drinking after school whenever he can get liquor, and it seems like he always can. He's going to be just like you, you know that?"

Probably every argument in the world has been tried by the children of addicts and alcoholics as they try frantically to find the right button that will send Mom or Dad to get help and break free.

When nothing works, the child too often thinks it is his fault, that somehow he or she should have been able to find the magic key that would make Mom or Dad suddenly decide to change.

Actually, strenuous effort on the part of a child can make the situation worse, not better, at least in some cases. The addicted parent interprets it as nagging (which it is). Most people, when nagged, tend to simply dig in their heels and become even more determined not to comply.

An addicted parent may think, or say out loud, "Blasted kid! What does he mean, I drink too much? I don't drink too much, and I resent his saying it. If he thinks he can make me give up a few relaxing drinks in the evening he's got another think coming." Or, "Little miss smartie pants! Who does she think she is, trying to run my life? I'll show her!" Or some other version that basically means, "He can talk until he's blue in the face. I don't intend to change one little bit."

Case Study: Ryan's father had always been a heavy drinker, but in the last two or three years Ryan had realized that the drinking was out of control and that his father passed out in a sodden stupor almost every weekend.

Ryan first tried to get his father interested in the things he used to like—playing football or softball with Ryan and some of the neighborhood guys. Dad didn't respond and became angry when Ryan pressed the issue.

Then Ryan tried pleading. "Come on, Dad, do it for us. We love you, and we worry about you." Total effect on Dad, zero.

Next up was guilt. "Mom's worried about the money you spend on booze and the time you lose from work. What's going to happen to us if you get fired? We'll wind up homeless, like the people you see on TV!"

The more Ryan tried, the angrier and more abusive his father became, until one night he backhanded Ryan through a glass patio door, which shattered, cutting him badly in several places. Stunned and bleeding, Ryan lay in the sea of broken glass as his father ranted and raved about what an awful son he was.

In the hospital Ryan finally told the doctor the whole story. The doctor recommended Alateen, the division of Alcoholics Anonymous for young people.

"But Dad won't go. I couldn't make him go. I've failed ."

"Son, you don't go to their meetings for your dad. You go for yourself. It's to help *you* cope with your dad's drinking problem."

At Alateen Ryan heard from other young people like himself about their efforts to make a parent stop drinking, and how they too felt guilty and like failures when they were unable to change him or her.

Oddly enough, as Ryan formed new friendships in the groups, became active in some of their projects, and got on with his life, his father began to realize that Ryan didn't seem to care anymore what happened, or at least not the way he once had. Realization penetrated his father's alcoholic haze that he was losing the son he really loved.

Eventually he joined Alcoholics Anonymous and did stop drinking.

Happy endings like that don't always happen, and certainly that had not been what the doctor had in mind when he recommended Alateen nor what Ryan had hoped for when he first joined. All he knew was that if he had gone on trying to get his father to stop, it almost certainly would never happened.

A child cannot change an addicted parent 999 times out of a thousand. Don't let yourself be drawn into feeling guilty or sad or depressed because of that. Get help for yourself and go on with your life.

CHAPTER 7

Effects on Your Nonusing Parent

The inner workings of a family that contains an addict or addicts are often very confusing to outsiders— *and* to some family members as well. It can best be described as a case of coaddiction.

The coaddict relationship is a *reciprocal relationship that is characterized by one person who behaves in an addicted manner and another who tries to control that person's addictive behavior.*

The following are the most commonly asked questions by those trying to understand the mechanics of coaddiction.

What Is a Coaddict?

Any person who has lived in an addicted family system could be correctly labeled a coaddict. Everyone in an addicted family system has been affected by the addict's use of a mood-altering drug. And all of them in their own ways make an adaptive response to the addict's behavior. These responses are attempts to control the stress in an extremely painful family situation.

More specifically, the spouse of an addict is the person in the family system who is usually identified as the coaddict.

Do Coaddicts Have Specific Traits By Which They Can Be Identified?

Yes. In fact, all coaddicts have a number of very similar personality traits. They also exhibit characteristic behavior patterns.

It makes little difference whether the coaddict is a child or an adult, a parent or a stepparent. Coaddiction is not dependent upon the addict's drug of choice.

What Are the Traits of a Coaddict?

The coaddict:

- has weak interpersonal boundaries
- is dependent
- denies the reality of his situation
- is controlling
- is obsessed
- has low self-worth
- practices caretaking
- is overly rigid
- does not stand up for himself
- does not leave the relationship when it is clear that the addict is violating the coaddict's values and has no intention of trying to change.

What Are "Weak Interpersonal Boundaries"?

Boundaries are the limits a person has set on his own or another person's behavior. Boundaries are of two types: personal and interpersonal. A personal boundary might be a decision never to participate in an extramarital affair. An interpersonal boundary might be a decision never to stay married to a spouse who is having an extramarital affair.

A personal boundary might be that you would probably keep money you found in the street but that you would never steal. An interpersonal boundary might be that you would not date or stay friends with a person who would steal.

Coaddicts often say that they would never tolerate a certain behavior, such as excessive drinking or the use of drugs, by another person. Yet when the other person exhibits that behavior, the coaddict stays in the relationship anyway.

Case Study: Renee's father is heavily into the use of cocaine. Her mother always covers up for him, telling the boss he is sick, making excuses, and so on. Renee despises them both for the way they are acting and what they are doing to each other and to her little brother and sister and herself.

Yet much the same situation is occurring in Renee's own life. Her friend Karin is putting her to the test about stealing. Renee would never steal anything, yet over and over after they had been shopping Renee would realize that Karin had been shoplifting. Renee said angrily that she did not want Karin to steal while they were in a store together. Yet two weeks later she saw Karin slipping a tube of mascara into her purse. Outside, Renee shouted furiously at her friend. Karin was upset and embarrassed and promised never to do it again.

Within days Renee again saw Karin stealing, slipping a bottle of perfume into a pocket. This time she told Karin point-blank that she would no longer be her friend if Karin continued to steal. Karin swore she would never do it again.

But before another week had passed Renee saw Karin slip a piece of jewelry into her purse. This time Renee said nothing.

While she hated the way her mother made things easy for her father in his addiction, she was slipping into exactly the same behavior pattern with her friend.

What Does "Dependent" Mean?

The dependent person has an inadequate sense of self. He or she seeks approval from others instead of making his or her own decisions. The dependent stays in relationships that don't work, that may even hurt. He or she is terrified of being abandoned and frequently allows others to abuse him or her. He puts his life on hold for other people.

Women and girls who believe that "You are nothing without a man," that it takes a man to "complete" you or your life, or who accept the words of the popular song "You're nobody 'til somebody loves you . . ." are mostly likely to be strongly dependent and to be hurt by that clinging dependence on someone else. But men can be dependent too.

Case Study: William's wife was characterized as "having a tongue that could clip a hedge," and Susie frequently turned her caustic comments on her husband, especially when she had been drinking. And that was often. Four to five nights a week she came home drunk, calling William ugly names.

William never answered back. He was afraid that if he made her angry she would leave him. He would be abandoned.

Late one Saturday night Susie came home so drunk that she couldn't get her key in the lock. William heard her stabbing at the door and cursing, so he opened the door for her.

"I've been worried about you," he said mildly. "I was afraid you might have been hurt in a car accident."

Susie focused on him blearily and said, "You poor, poor pitiful man. You have nothing more important to do than wring your hands and worry about me. What would you ever do if you had to live by yourself?"

William didn't answer but just stood looking cowed. He had tears in his eyes, but he didn't respond to his wife's acidity.

"If you were any kind of a man, I wouldn't need to drink. I think I'll just go back to the bar. At least there are intelligent people there to talk to, not a sniveling little wimp."

"Please," begged William, "you've had too much to drink to be able to drive."

His wife just sneered as she staggered back to her car. William went back into the house without another word.

Often, and frequently without being aware that they are doing it, dependent people *encourage* addictive or other destructive behavior in a spouse. They reason: "If he really drinks too much, I can help protect him from the consequences. He will *need* me. That way he'll never want to leave."

Or, "I really wish my wife would lose some weight. But if she did she might be attractive enough to other men that one would take her away from me, and I couldn't stand that. She's so happy with this new diet—think I'll go out and get her a giant pizza and some ice cream. I'll tell her just once won't hurt."

That explains, to some degree, the situation that so many children of addicts find so confusing: On the one hand, Mom is always after Dad to quit drinking so much and complains about what his drinking is doing to all of them. Yet on the other hand for his birthday she buys him a fancy decanter of expensive whiskey.

How Do Coaddicts Deny the Reality of Their Situation?

Coaddicts become very good at denying many things. They deny that their "significant other"—a boyfriend or girlfriend or a spouse—is addicted. They deny that their children are being abused. They deny that they are unhappy, that they themselves have been abused.

They deny that they have feelings. They deny the embarrassment caused by their spouse's addiction. They deny that the spouse's addiction is tearing the family apart, leaving their children with deep emotional scars.

Case Study: Reginald's wife is addicted to alcohol and occasionally uses drugs. She is frequently abusive to their children, once breaking the youngest girl's arm when she threw her against a wall in an alcoholic rage. She is frequently hostile to Reginald and sometimes attacks him physically.

Yet to outsiders Reginald says things like, "This has been a truly great year. The Lord has blessed us abundantly. He has given me a good wife and great children. And it is remarkable how well we get along together."

Reginald has just made this speech to the Sunday School class he teaches. As they leave the classroom, one of his friends says to Reginald, "You really are lucky to have a family that get along. In my family we fight over trivial matters far too often. I wish we didn't fight so much. It sure would make life better."

Reginald didn't notice his son walking behind him as he replied, "That really is a shame. I wish there were a way I could help you and your family get along better. My wife and I used to fight sometimes, but we stopped that years ago."

Reggie Jr. is thunderstruck. The fight between his parents the previous night had ended with Mom bopping Dad over the head with a skillet and he himself getting knocked over a chair when he tried to break it up. His back and ribs still hurt. Mom and Dad had screamed at each other for hours even after they quit hitting.

Reggie Jr. knows he is living in a nightmare, yet hearing his father talk like that and knowing the truth is making him doubt his own perception of what is and is not real.

How Are Coaddicts Controlling?

A coaddict tries to control the addict's drinking or using and generally goes from that to trying to control his life and sometimes the lives of the children. He or she pours out liquor, flushes drugs down the toilet, hides money so that the addict cannot buy more alcohol or drugs.

The coaddict may keep on trying to control the addict's life so there is no opportunity to buy drugs. If that is impossible, and it generally is, he or she may go on to demand tyrannical control of the children's lives, just to feel in control of *something*.

Case Study: Carmelita's dad is an alcoholic. For the last two or three years her mother has been searching the house every day for liquor and pouring what she finds down the sink. Lately she has taken to driving her husband to work, meeting him for lunch as often as possible, and driving him home at night. She hopes in this way to keep him from buying liquor.

It isn't working, and her parents are fighting more and more as her dad drinks more and more. Lately Mom has stepped up her efforts to control her family. She calls her husband four or five times a day at work and insists on going with him whenever he leaves the house at night.

All that is bad enough and seems to be making Dad drink more. But lately Mom has begun acting the same way to Carmelita and her brothers. Mom demands to know where they are at all times, whom they are with, what they are doing.

Rules have become more rigid. For example, they are supposed to be home no later than twenty minutes after school is out. One day Carmelita called to say that they were having cheerleader tryouts and she was going to try. Mom interrupted with a furious order to be home in twenty minutes or else.

Rules make prisoners of the children. Carmelita may *not* wear her skirt more than one inch above or below her kneecap. She may not date until she is sixteen, and that means not even walking to the neighborhood movie with the boy next door who is a year younger than she is but a good friend.

Carmelita and her brothers are right—the rules don't make a lot of sense. They are Mom's way of trying to control *some* aspects of a family situation that she correctly sees as getting away from her and heading for a total smash.

What Is "Caretaking"?

Caretaking is being overly responsible, doing things for other people that they could and should do for themselves.

Coaddicts are often so overly responsible that they give away opportunities to have their own needs met. They wind up overcommitted, feeling other people's problems more deeply than do the people themselves. They feel more comfortable giving than receiving and offer advice when it is not wanted or needed.

Like the very dependent person, they need to be "needed."

Case Study: Kevin is fourteen. He and his friends were watching television when he suddenly had an attack of the sneezes. His mother, who happened to be walking through the den at the moment, pulled a tissue from a box and wiped Kevin's nose. It embarrassed him a great deal. "Mom," he said, in protest, "I'm old enough to do that myself!"

"I'm sorry—I guess to me you'll always be my little boy."

"Mom, I'm not your little boy! I'm fourteen. Come on, give me a break!"

Kevin's mother's eyes filled with tears. "Nobody seems to want me anymore."

Later Mom asked about Kevin's homework. "Yes, I have some homework," Kevin said, digging it out of his backpack.

"Can I help you with it, honey?"

"Not now. This is easy." Again with tears threatening, Mom went to the kitchen to begin clearing up. But soon she stopped and began to fix Kevin an elaborate snack.

"Here, honey," she said, "I've fixed you something to

snack on while you do your homework, since I don't seem to be able to help you any other way."

"Mom, it wasn't necessary. This really isn't hard and won't take long. Besides, we just finished dinner and I'm not hungry. Why are you always doing things for me that I can do for myself? Don't you trust me to be able to take care of myself or know what I want or need?"

Kevin's mother left the room quickly with tears in her eyes. She then decided to find Kevin's sister and see how she could take care of her.

What Is Obsession?

Coaddicts often become obsessed about unimportant details. They spend much time and energy dealing with other people's problems. They try to catch others doing something wrong. They frequently worry about another's behavior. Sometimes they are unable to sleep worrying about what someone else has done, or might do.

They focus on another person to the point of ignoring things that should be important to themselves.

Case Study: Harold's wife was an alcoholic. He was obsessed with controlling her drinking. He had been taking her to work, having lunch with her, and picking her up after work for over a year. He spent almost every waking moment with her during the weekends.

One night while she was cooking dinner she said to Harold, "We're out of bread, honey, and we need some for dinner."

At this simple statement Harold felt his pulse race. "How will I handle this?" he thought, with something akin to panic. "She can't quit cooking because the boys have to eat. If I cook dinner and she goes to the store, she may stop on the way and buy a bottle. If I leave her here alone while I go to the store, she may drink. I know what to do! I'll mark the level of whiskey in the bottle. That way, I'll know if she takes a drink."

Harold sped to the nearest convenience store, grabbed a loaf of bread, rushed to the front of the check-out line and dropped two dollars on the counter, saying, "Keep the change!"

He sped home and ran into the house. His wife was calmly at work in the kitchen. He handed her the bread and headed for the den, where he checked the whiskey bottle. Not a drop was missing, and he felt a great sense of relief.

But back in the kitchen he realized that his wife was acting as if she had been drinking. He couldn't figure it out. None of the whiskey was gone, but she sure seemed to have had something to drink.

He began to search the house. No other bottles were to be found. Harold began to wonder if he were losing his mind. What Harold didn't know was that his wife knew about the mark on the whiskey bottle. She had poured a glass of whiskey and drunk it, then carefully filled the bottle to the pencil line with tea.

Harold felt even more obsessed with his wife and her drinking. Now he had to know whether or not he was crazy. That night he couldn't sleep worrying about ways to increase his vigilance.

What Harold had not seen was that his preoccupation with his wife was putting his job at risk, and that his oldest son was smoking marijuana on a steadily increasing basis.

How Do Codependents Fail to Stand Up for Themselves?

They allow others to control their behavior. They allow themselves to be criticized unjustly and frequently play down their own abilities. They allow themselves to be treated unfairly and to be victimized by others.

They are judgmental and harsh with themselves, and yet they are also afraid to ask important questions—questions they think might rock the boat. They are too sensitive. Their lives are filled with self-imposed "shoulds"—"I should do this," "I should have done that and I know things would have been better if I'd had the sense to do it," "Tomorrow, instead of concentrating on my job, I should . . ." And so on and so on. All others' needs come before their own.

Case Study: Bill is addicted to speed, although he will use just about any drug he can get his hands on. His marriage is very shaky because of debts, the increasingly shabby dump where the family lives, and his failure to hold a job. This is his second marriage. He has custody of his son, Mark.

According to Bill, all their problems are the fault of his wife, Susan. When he missed a date with his connection to buy drugs and began to go into withdrawal, he was furious with Susan. He screamed at her because she had taken the car to apply for a job and was gone an hour and a half. Instead of replying, "The big boss wanted to talk to me. I couldn't very well walk out if I wanted the job, could I?" Susan said nothing.

When he blamed their bills and debts on her "wild spending" (she had just spent $30 on much needed new clothes for the new job), she didn't point out that he was spending hundreds a week on drugs.

In fact, she did blame herself, certain that if she were "a good wife" Bill wouldn't act as he did and would be able to kick his habit.

Finally she began to see, and tried to point out to Bill, that Mark was beginning to act just like his father. Nothing that went wrong in his life was his fault. He could always blame someone else.

One morning Bill and Mark woke up and found Susan gone. After five years of browbeating and failure to take up for herself, Susan had realized it was time, and past time, to split.

How Can a Coaddict Know When It Is Time to Leave?

It is important for a coaddict to decide what he or she is willing to live with and what his or her bottom line is. Once those things are decided, he or she should be willing to take action according to that bottom line. That could include leaving the relationship, as Susan did.

Case Study: Cybil was in the kitchen one day when her husband came home from work for lunch. Cybil greeted him with, "I have given a lot of thought to this situation with our son Neal. I have come to realize that I can no longer handle having him in the house overnight. It worries me when he picks on his sisters and slaps and punches them when he is high on drugs and liquor. I worry that he'll decide to cook himself a meal in the middle of the night and burn the house down.

"And I worry about you, that he is going to push you to the point of beating the daylights out of him when he comes around pickled to the gills on booze or gooned out on drugs. I don't want to see you in jail, honey. It scared the daylights out of me when he came over the other night acting like a wild man and you told me later you had started looking for your handgun as a way of dealing with him when he was out of control.

"The next time he asks to move back in, or even stay overnight, please respect my decision on this. He's welcome to visit, but not to stay."

Conner hugged his wife and said, "Okay, honey. I understand, and I'll back you up all the way."

The next evening Cybil and Conner had just come home from a movie when Neal rang the doorbell. Cybil greeted her son but noticed that his eyes were dilated and that he smelled strongly of liquor. They invited him in and visited for a few minutes. Cybil asked Neal if she could get him anything to eat or help him in any way. Each time he said, "No."

Cybil could no longer stand it and finally asked where he was staying that night.

He looked surprised and said, "Why, right here, in my room."

Cybil shook her head. "Neal, I discussed this situation with your dad yesterday and explained to him that I worry too much when you stay overnight in the house. Decide where you want to go, or we'll help you find a place."

Conner looked unhappy. "Cybil, we can't make him leave. One more night in the house isn't going to make that much difference."

Cybil was hurt but mustered her courage and said, "It would hurt me. If Neal is going to stay the night here, then I'm not. If that's the way it has to be, I'll get the girls and go to a motel.

"Neal, I love you and always will, but I can't stay in the same house overnight with you again. I'm always glad to have you visit, and I'd help you in any way possible. We all would, you know that!

"You get high to make yourself feel better. Now I'm going to have to do something to make *me* feel better when you are using and high, or drunk, or all of the above."

(As you can see, there is a great deal of overlapping of the reactions to and types of behavior involved in alcoholism and addiction.)

What Is the Coaddict Cycle? Why Would Anyone Want to Stay in a Miserable Situation?

People stay because at first not all of it is miserable. In fact, at first the rewards may be pretty good.

The coaddict cycle is very much like the addict cycle. It simply runs in the opposite direction:

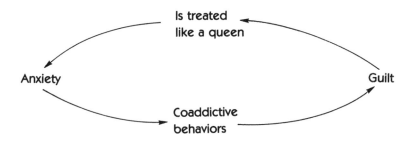

Case Study: Gary wonders how his parents' relationship ever got into such a mess, with his mom an alcoholic and his dad close to a nervous breakdown because of it. He has no idea what things were like when they first began dating.

In those days, on Saturday nights, Sylvia's main interest

was in "partying." She generally did this by calling a group of friends and making plans to go dancing. The partying always included a lot of drinking, and Sylvia always wanted her boyfriend, Gene, in on it.

Gene became a coaddict. When they went out together with her friends, Gene felt on top of the world. Sylvia would compliment him in front of other people, build him up, make him feel important. She let everyone know how great Gene was to be with and that no one could measure up to him as a man. Sylvia loved to dance in a way that got her a lot of attention, with moves that might have come off a floor show in Las Vegas. After a few drinks she and Gene usually put on a real show on the dance floor.

After a Saturday night out with Sylvia, Gene would think a lot about their evening together, about how other men had looked at her, and he would begin to worry. He concluded that if he couldn't be around Sylvia all the time, she might drop him and start seeing another man.

The next time they were out Gene was determined to stay with Sylvia all the time. She found him "hanging" on her the whole evening, even to the point of deciding when they would go to the restrooms. He became very short with the people around him, most of them her friends.

"Why don't you just relax?" Sylvia asked, a little short herself. "You aren't any fun when you are so uptight. Back off a little, you are embarrassing me!"

Gene began to feel bad that he wasn't trusting Sylvia. He answered, "Maybe you're right, Sylvia. I just find myself so jealous, and I know that all the men in the room would like to be with you." Sylvia responded by focusing on him totally, making him feel very special and important.

Gene's addiction to Sylvia merely grew with her addiction to alcohol.

How Is the Addict's Cycle Related to the Coaddict's Cycle?

The addict's cycle tends to fit hand in glove with the coaddict's cycle. The cycles reinforce each other in very subtle ways. The addict and coaddict keep each other sick. They need each other to maintain their addiction.

That is why you so often hear of someone divorcing an alcoholic and promptly marrying another alcoholic. It happens all the time.

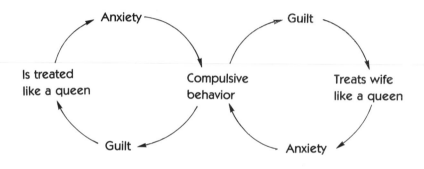

Case Study: Gregory was recently discharged from a chemical dependency center after successful treatment for addiction to cocaine. His wife, Annette, had participated in the treatment center's family program. Since his discharge, however, Annette had felt a growing sense of dissatisfaction.

Something was very different about Gregory now. He didn't mistreat her, but what she wanted was for him to treat her as he had in the past when he wasn't strung out on drugs.

At those times he was overcome with guilt and self-blame and would try to make up to her for whatever he had done in his last drug-using episode. Then Gregory had treated her like a queen. And Annette had thought that that was how he would behave all the time now that he wasn't using drugs.

The hitch was that now Gregory wasn't feeling guilty about anything, so he was just being himself.

Annette didn't quite know what to do. She finally realized that she had known Gregory the drug addict for so long that she didn't know Gregory the recovering addict at all. She also had no sense of what it should be like to be in a relationship with someone who wasn't using drugs.

All of this made Annette extremely uncomfortable and anxious. She began to wonder if Gregory were having an affair. To find out, she decided to follow him to and from work.

On the third day Gregory caught her, and she offered a not very believable excuse. "I was just bringing you your briefcase."

"Well, where is it, then?"

"Can you believe it ? I followed you all the way downtown to bring the briefcase to you and I forgot to put it in the car."

Gregory stared at her. "Of course, you forgot to put it in the car because my briefcase is already in *my* car. Sometimes you drive me crazy, Annette. I think you were just following me."

Annette denied that. Later Gregory began to wonder if she were following him to make sure he actually was at work before she set out to meet a boyfriend.

The couple's three teenagers became caught up in the tangle of mistrust, suspicion, lack of communication, and misunderstood motives. Before long Gregory was back on drugs again.

Who Is More Obsessed, the Addict or the Coaddict?

While the addict is obsessed with using and the coaddict is obsessed with the addict's not using, both end up obsessed. The only difference is that the addict is addicted to a mood-altering substance or behavior, and the coaddict is addicted to the addict.

Sound complicated? It is—and it isn't. The bottom line is that both persons will place their jobs, religion, finances, social lives, and children second to their individual addictions.

Case Study: Edna is the wife of Wayne, a successful businessman, who has a very expensive cocaine addiction. She hates his drug use and the types of people he deals with to get drugs.

She also hates dealing with creditors and making excuses when she must cover their inability to pay their bills. She hurts when she faces the children after she has had to sell something to make ends meet. She finds herself making excuses to her friends about absent furniture and possessions, when it is obvious that their expensive home is becoming more and more bare. She is beginning to find herself avoiding contact with many people outside of the family.

One day she confronted her husband. "Wayne, I want you to realize that we are about to lose this house. You don't get paid for two more weeks, and I don't see how we can make it until then. There isn't another thing I can sell or pawn. If you don't get off cocaine, we are all going down the tube."

Wayne hung his head and mumbled. He had been feeling terribly guilty about his drug use, what it was doing to their children, how it was affecting his life and threatening his career. A week earlier he had begun attending meetings of Narcotics Anonymous, although he didn't want to tell his wife; he had always refused to admit that he had a problem.

The next day he came home all smiles and handed her a roll of bills—enough to catch up on their payments and have some left over to get through the month. He also took her out to dinner at a nice restaurant.

Edna's feeling of relief was short-lived, however. She knew that the money couldn't have been from her husband's paycheck, and their savings were long gone. She had heard about addicts turning to crime, and she was paralyzed with fear that Wayne had robbed a store or something.

Wayne was too ashamed to tell her that he had bought cocaine for a friend while the man was out of work for a month, and the friend had just paid him back.

Soon Edna was searching Wayne's clothes and wallet, asking him pointed questions, obviously doubting the answers. And so the cycle began again . . .

How Does the Coaddict Inadvertently Keep the Cycle Going?

The coaddict enables the addict to continue practicing his addiction, rather than the other way around, by protecting him from the consequences of his behavior. When he is drunk she calls his boss and says that he is sick. She turns down dinner invitations if she knows alcohol will be served. She makes excuses for his behavior.

When he drinks up his paycheck, she pawns her jewelry and makes excuses to creditors.

In these and many other ways she acts as a buffer for

the addict. In her attempts to "help," she insures that the addict will continue to drink or use.

Case Study: Laurel was very concerned about Terrance's drug use. She was afraid that he would lose his job. She was afraid that he couldn't pay the rent. She was afraid that her family would find out. She was afraid that *his* family would find out. She was afraid of what the kids would think.

In fact, she was afraid of everything.

In efforts to manage her own fear, her life became a frantic, nonstop effort to protect Terrance and herself from the consequences exposure might bring.

Terrance came home late one night, stoned. Even though his mother had called and said it was important, Laurel did not give him the message. She was afraid he would return the call at 2:30 a.m. and his mother would find out the condition he was in.

The next morning he was too sick to go to work; Laurel called in and said he had the flu. She hocked her wedding ring and some jewelry that had been her grandmother's to pay the rent.

Terrance never had to confront the problems his drug use was creating for them all because Laurel was so good at protecting him.

Six months later Terrance overdosed and was rushed to the hospital in a coma. He died a week later.

It was only then that Laurel began to see, dimly, that all her protecting of him might have been a big mistake, might have contributed to his death.

How Does the Coaddict Trigger a Relapse?

The coaddict and the addict tend to get locked into a game that could be called "Cops and Robbers." The coaddict is the "cop" who tries to police the addict's behavior. The addict tries to elude the coaddict's attempts at control. Round and round and round they go in a shatteringly destructive "dance/war."

If they are to stop this self-defeating game, they both have to change at the same time. All one-sided changes are destined to fail.

If the coaddict decides to trust the addict and if the addict continues to practice his addiction, he may sell her wedding ring for drugs. If the addict decides to quit using, the controlling behavior of the coaddict will convince him that he is untrustworthy and hopelessly guilty. He will then use to feel better about himself.

The situation often exists when the addict returns from treatment. He is no longer using. He is no longer practicing guilt-motivated behaviors such as "treating her like a queen."

What she wants is for him to be the way he was when he wasn't using but was feeling guilty. So she begins to stir up the guilt . . . "You never seem to care about me anymore," or "You spend as much time at work as you ever did at the bar."

That triggers his feelings of guilt. That in turn sets up his using again.

That is why it is *vital* for the coaddict to get treatment, too. Otherwise nothing is likely to change for the better permanently.

CHAPTER 8

What Should I Tell My Friends?

O
ne of the many problems of children of addicted parents is the isolation that they feel. If one gets too close to other people, one might let slip— family secrets.

In these families, of course, a major part of the energy is invested in keeping secrets, not letting anyone know about Mom's little problem, Dad's little weakness. The parents may be pillars of the community, important business or professional people. Woe to the child who cracks the facade.

Case Study: The book *Bad Blood* by Richard M. Levine is the true story of a sixteen-year-old California girl, Marlene. She was the daughter of an alcoholic mother and a wimpy, indecisive father who protected his wife from the effects of her drinking and refused to make any effort to deal with it or the problems it was causing.

Family life had been a running battle between parents

and daughter for years, and Marlene genuinely made attempts to get help. But when the family went for counseling or tried to deal with the problems with the law that Marlene's behavior was causing, and Marlene mentioned her mother's drinking, that invariably ended things and Marlene caught blazes for "washing our dirty linen in public."

Unable to stop the cycle or handle it, Marlene finally goaded her twenty-year-old boyfriend into murdering her mother and father.

Telling friends about your problems at home could have a number of consequences, from very positive to very negative. It is usually a matter of using your own best judgment.

It is possible that your friends already have an idea of what is wrong and for your sake haven't said anything. If they show that they know and are not going to judge you or cause problems, sometimes talking can bring a tremendous sense of relief. You might even find that friends have had similar problems in their lives.

But let's be honest. You could also lose friends because of your parents' problem.

Case Study: Jennifer and Mark had begun dating in their junior year in high school and liked each other a lot. They planned to go to the same university and even wanted to major in similar subjects. Mark felt a little humble that Jennifer dated him—she was one of the prettiest girls in school, as well as the daughter of a district judge and quite well off.

One afternoon, over snacks at a fast-food place, Jennifer asked casually about Mark's mother's moods. Mark had taken Jennifer to his house a few times, and his mother's mood swings had struck her as odd. About half the time she reacted as if Jennifer were a total stranger.

Mark did something very unusual—he told Jennifer that his mother was an alcoholic, that she was usually "knee-walking drunk" by noon, and that his family had managed to hide it from the world.

Jennifer was somewhat thrown by the information, but she didn't condemn Mark because of it. However, she telephoned him three days later in tears. She had told her little sister, and the little sister had passed it on to Dear Old Dad, who promptly forbade Jennifer to see Mark again.

"He said, 'What would people think?' and that you might turn out like that and a bunch of other nonsense," Jennifer wailed. "He wouldn't listen to a thing I said. He was really *awful* about it!"

Mark was devastated. His fear of turning out like his mother was so great that he had never so much as taken a sip of beer. Hearing this from Jennifer's stuffed shirt of a father was just too much.

Yet Jennifer's father's reaction is not uncommon. As many adult children of alcoholics can tell you, the stigma of being the son or daughter of "the town drunk" can last all your life.

Case Study: Caryn and Collette met when they were five and their families moved next door to each other. Although Caryn's family moved to another part of town when they were in the sixth grade, the girls remained best friends. Their birthdays were two weeks apart, and, because of the similarity in names, they joked that one birth certificate was in error and they were actually twins separated at birth.

Certainly they were as close as sisters, and in all the

time they had known each other they had never had a serious disagreement.

The summer they turned sixteen Caryn pressed Collette to tell her what was wrong. She knew something was worrying her friend, and she felt sure it was something serious.

Somewhat reluctantly Collette did tell her. She had known for the past three or four years that her parents had been snorting cocaine now and then, on a "recreational" basis, she guessed they called it.

But about six months ago her father's company encountered some very serious business problems, and as his worries increased, so did his cocaine use. Now it was beginning to affect his behavior, the family finances, and his performance on the job. Collette was really frightened that her father might be becoming an addict.

Caryn was flabbergasted. She had no idea what to say. Her family was very religious, extremely strict in their beliefs. Caryn was not permitted to wear shorts in public, go to school dances, or attend other churches. She had once confided in Collette that she considered drug use "almost as bad a sin as murder."

Now she couldn't handle what Collette had told her. Over the next few weeks Collette saw her friend gradually pull away, ease out of the almost lifelong friendship.

"She was going places with other people, not returning my phone calls or making excuses not to talk to me, avoiding me at school."

The effect on Collette was devastating. "It was as if I weren't good enough for her anymore, as if what my parents did made *me* a less good person. I had been feeling not too great about myself before, but that just pushed me over the edge. By the end of that summer, between problems at home and being dumped by my best friend for something over which I had no control, I was thinking seriously of suicide. It was like losing a sister. I had no idea something could hurt that much."

Case Study: Alleta and Kerry were good friends, although neither considered the other a "best friend." So Alleta wasn't sure exactly why she invited Kerry to stop by her house one day and pick up a book she had promised to lend Kerry.

Although her parents were wealthy and considered among the town's leading "socialites," four or five times a week Alleta came home to find her mother passed out from drinking. On this particular day Mom was in her bedroom, and Alleta could tell from the snores that drifted down the stairs that she had been hitting the bottle again.

Alleta got the book and then abruptly blurted out to Kerry their "family problem" and the effect it was having on her father, older sister, and two little brothers.

Kerry stared at her. "Oh, man, do I know what you mean! *Exactly* what you mean," Kerry said, and then told Alleta about her alcohol- *and* drug-using father, who beat family members and more than once had had to be bailed out of jail for fights, drug possession, and once a robbery.

"Mom divorced him when I was twelve—I've never been so thankful for anything in my life. Mom started me going to Alateen when I was eleven, and that was what held me together and helped me get over Dad. I still go now and then. I'll go with you, if you want. It'll help, I promise."

It did help. Alleta found sympathy, understanding, freedom to express her feelings, and explanations of some of the things her mother did and the way they made her feel and react.

From being casual friends, Alleta and Kerry have

become very close, helping each other with a mutual problem that still now and then troubles their lives.

Telling your friends (if they don't already know) does have its risks, as shown by the case studies. It could improve your life or genuinely mar it. Use your own best judgment in the matter of whom you talk to.

But do go to Alateen. These meetings, for the children of alcoholics and addicts, will give you a chance to talk, to express what is going on in your life and how it is affecting you. Alateen will not help you to change a parent's behavior; as has been said before, that is difficult if not impossible for a child to do.

What Alateen does is help you to cope with your own feelings, your own reactions to your parents' problems.

It gives you friends who do understand, really understand.

As Lori, fifteen, puts it, "I have to sneak around even to go to the meetings. When I once mentioned wanting to go, my folks raised the roof. They said they didn't have a drinking problem and they weren't going to have everybody in town thinking that they did. They are both boozers and just won't admit it.

"But once I started going to the meetings I found out that even that wasn't unusual. A lot of the kids said their parents refused to admit that anything was wrong. They felt just the way I did about it.

"One of the big problems, living the way I did, was that you feel so cut off from other people. My folks didn't encourage me to have friends over, and I sure didn't push it. Who wants to bring in a friend when you might find your mother sitting on the couch in her underwear, whacked out of her mind?

"I knew my home life wasn't like most kids, and I didn't

feel like most kids. I felt—I don't know—marked by what my folks are like, and scarrred by it in some way.

"But at Alateen I found that I wasn't alone, that there wasn't something wrong with me or my feelings. I found a lot of kids who felt just the same way. If my feelings were normal, maybe I wasn't a weirdo after all.

"I found friends who *understand*—I can't tell you how much that has meant to me."

CHAPTER 9

How It Affects Family Relationships

C hildren who live with two parents who abuse drugs, or with one parent who abuses drugs and another parent who is codependent, often feel as if they are living in a tornado. Everything is mixed up, confusing, and very frightening.

Part of the time they may be taking care of their parents when their parents should be taking care of them. They may be afraid to invite friends home because they can never be sure if their parents will be sober, embarrassing, or abusive.

These children live tremendously stressful and painful lives. They may attempt to control their stress and pain by limiting the number of choices they have to make about how to act. In fact, their lives may be so turbulent that their own behavior is the only thing that is under control.

This causes them to limit their responses to life. Exactly how they do this depends on how at least one other family member acts. Eventually their behavior develops and is maintained in stereotypical roles. In other words, each of these roles are reciprocal. They happen because of someone else's behavior. So, as we describe them, we shall do so in pairs—"reciprocal pairs"—together with the roles that create them.

Turtle—Grand Inquisitor Relationships

Did you ever notice how some kids "turtle up" when they get in trouble? They just sit there and refuse to say a word. There is a reason for this: They are in a relationship with someone who is behaving like a Grand Inquisitor.

Originally, Grand Inquisitors were people sent out by the church to find heretics (people who didn't believe what the church told them) and witches (people the church thought were worshiping the devil). When Grand Inquisitors found people they thought might be heretics or witches, they would question or test them. The problem was that they frequently asked "double-bind" questions or used double-bind tests. These are questions and tests designed in such a way that however the person answers, he is guilty.

An example of such questions is, "Do you still worship the devil?" Whether the person answered yes or no, he was guilty. To say anything other than yes or no was a sign of noncooperation, which meant that the person was a witch. An example of a test was to tie a suspect's hands and feet and throw her into a lake. If she came to the surface, it meant that she was a witch, since only people who practiced witchcraft could manage to swim with their hands and feet tied. Witches were put to death.

Kids who live with a grand inquisitor are asked things like "Are you as lazy as your brother?" If they say yes, they are admitting that they are lazy, which means Dad will hit them for it. If they say no, their brother will hit them for implying that he is lazy. Or they will be asked in front of friends, "You still delivering newspapers?" If they say no, they will be accused of being lazy. If they say yes, they will be thought stupid for working for so little money. Either way, they will be criticized in front of their friends.

Case Study: Roberto had finished his homework, cooked dinner, and had just turned on the television when his father came home from the office. "Sitting on your behind as usual," he sneered.

"I am not," said Roberto. "I just . . ."

"Don't back-talk me, you smart-mouth brat!" said his father.

"I wasn't back-talking. I was . . ."

With that his father started toward him with his fist raised. "You'll never learn to shut your mouth, will you?" he said.

Three weeks later, his father got a call from the principal. "Your son has been accused of cheating on a test. I didn't believe it, at first. But I've asked him about it over and over, and he won't tell me a thing."

"I'll beat him black and blue! No kid of mine is going to be a cheat."

"Mr. Mendez, I don't know that he cheated, but he won't talk to me. We always seemed to get along well. I just don't know what to make of this."

"He always does that when he's done something wrong."

said Mr. Mendez. "But don't worry.! I'll take care of Mr. Cheater!"

Because turtles are damned if they do and damned if they don't, they figure the smartest thing they can do is to say nothing. Sometimes a grand inquisitor may become distracted or forget. It's a turtle's only chance of escape. Unfortunately, others may mistake their silence for an admission of guilt.

Parentified Child—Incompetent Parent Relationships

Parentified children are kids who behave more like parents than like children. They do so because at least one of their parents behaves incompetently. This forces the child—and these "kids" can be twenty—to take over the parent's role.

There are many reasons why a parent may behave incompetently. He or she may be disabled by accident or illness. He or she may be single, or working two jobs. The parent might be in the military, or in prison, and be away from home for extended periods of time. Whenever a parent is unable or unwilling to be a parent in the fullest sense, his or her child is forced into a parentified role.

For our purposes, the parent's incompetency is caused by alcohol or other drug abuse. This represents a special case because the parent is usually in the home but unavailable emotionally and sometimes physically. It also means that the parentified role is permanent (unless the parent receives treatment and resumes the parental role). Children usually try to hide a parent's addiction. This caused the child to perform the parentified role while pretending that everything is fine.

Case Study: Georgina's father was "doing time" for smuggling cocaine. Her mother was an alcoholic who worked two jobs to support her family and her drinking habit. Georgina was the second child, but her older brother was strung out on heroin and completely unreliable. This left Georgina to care for her three little sisters.

Every weekday morning she got them up and dressed, fixed breakfast, washed the dishes, and took them out to meet the bus. She could never be sure when her mother would get home, because sometimes she stopped at a bar. Several times recently she hadn't come home at all.

One morning, Georgina awoke to find her mother asleep in her clothes on the couch. The smell of liquor was so strong that it made Georgina sick. "Wake up, Mama," she shouted, "you're late for work!"

"I'm too tired. Leave me alone."

"But, Mama, we need the money! The rent is due, and the man called to say they would shut off the electricity if we don't pay the bill by Monday."

"Okay, damn it! I'll go to work," said her mother as she got up and staggered toward the bathroom. She noticed the coffee table too late.

"Look out, Mama!" cried Georgina as her mother fell. She rushed to help her up. "Are you all right, Mama?"

"Hell, yes, I'm all right," she muttered. "You think I'm too drunk to get to work, don't you?"

"Of course not, Mama. You can always get to work," Georgina lied. Secretly, she was very worried. Her mother was in no shape to be driving the car. She might have an accident, maybe even be killed. Georgina had to think of a way to stop her. "Mama, come lie down. I need to talk to you," she said. Her mother walked unsteadily to the bedroom and sat down heavily on the bed. "Lie back,

Mama. Here, cover up and stay warm. I'll get the kids up, and then we'll talk. All right?"

"All right," said her mother. She was asleep in seconds. Georgina grabbed her mother's purse, took out the car keys, and put them on top of the refrigerator. Then she rushed the kids through breakfast and out to meet the bus.

At school, she went directly to the principal's office, asked to use the phone, and called her mother's office. "Hello," she said, "This is Georgina, Kay Johnson's daughter? Yes. She has the flu. No, she's much too sick to talk! Thanks, I'll tell her."

Parentified children live very stressful lives. They are not prepared for the responsibilities they are forced to accept. Eventually, they lose the ability to be children. Their lives are just too serious. Most suffer from long-term anxiety and depression. They also have trouble learning to trust others. These problems may last a lifetime without professional help.

Warrior—Peacemaker Relationships

The relationship between the warrior and the peacemaker is more complicated than most people ever guess. The peacemaker is openly trying to protect the warrior from someone, while the warrior is secretly trying to protect the peacemaker at the same time.

Case Study: Ricky had always started fights with his brother, Larry, who was two years older and much bigger. You would think there would have been only one fight that was over very quickly, with Larry having severely beaten Ricky. But that never happened, because their mother always stepped in before Ricky got hurt.

Larry thought that Ricky picked fights only when their mother was present. He assumed this was because Ricky knew that she would protect him. That was only half true. In fact, Ricky started fights only when both their mother and father were there. He would pick a fight whenever their parents got close to discussing their father's drinking.

One evening during dinner their father, who owned a service station, said, "I've got to run a load of gas cans down to Joe Dory's place." He pushed back from the table and started to get up.

"Just a minute," said their mother. "I'll go with you!"

"You can't," said their father. "The seat's full of tools I'll need tomorrow. Don't worry, I'll be back in an hour."

"Sure you will," she said, "just like you'll always be right back. You'll stop off at the Black Cat for a drink, just like always. Then you'll come home drunk, just like always . . ."

She turned just in time to see Ricky dump his glass of milk on Larry's head. Larry grabbed Ricky by his shirt with one hand and was dragging him across the table. His other hand was a fist ready to punch Ricky in the face.

"Stop!" screamed their mother as she grabbed Larry's arm. "You'll hurt him! He's just a child!"

"Hurt him?" shouted Larry, struggling to get his hand free, "I'm gonna break his face!"

"No, you're not!" said their mother, holding on for all she was worth. "Let him go! Now!"

"Okay," said Larry, "I'll let the little jackass go!" With that he pushed Ricky's face into the table as hard as he could. Then he let go.

"Ahhhh!" Ricky screamed as pain hit him. Then his knees buckled and he fell to the floor.

"Oh, no," said their mother as she ran to Ricky and picked him up. Then, seeing blood running down his face, she said to Larry, "Now look what you've done! You're nothing but a bully!"

Their father said to their mother, "You take care of Ricky. I'll take Larry with me. Looks like he could use some time to cool off." Then to Larry he said sternly, "You better come with me. Get your coat."

Larry looked at his mother as he left. She was sitting on the couch with Ricky's head in her lap, lovingly wiping his face with a warm washcloth. Ricky contentedly grinned up at him.

It was always the same. Dad would hit Larry a few times for hurting Ricky and upsetting their mother. After the gas cans were delivered, they'd stop at the Black Cat, where Larry would play video games while Dad drank. When he was so drunk that he fell off the bar stool, Larry would drive him home and help his mother put him to bed. At that point, she would tell Larry that she was proud of him for taking care of his father.

Living with a peacemaker and a warrior makes everyone feel as if they are losing their mind. No one ever seems to figure out what's wrong. And so it continues!

Hero—Rebel Relationships

Heroes are kids who try to take the stress off the family by doing something very well. They may be the quarterback of the football team, or the head cheerleader, or the church youth group leader, or a straight-A student, or all of the above. They'll do whatever it takes. Soon the entire family is bragging about the hero. In the face of that performance, the drug-abusing parent and his or her behavior are temporarily forgotten.

Rebels are kids who try to take the stress off the family by doing something wrong. They may get into trouble at school, or shoplift, or steal a car, or get drunk and thrown into jail, or all of the above. Soon the entire family is worrying about the rebel. In the face of that performance, the drug-abusing parent and his or her behavior are temporarily forgotten.

Case Study: Therese's teachers were confused. She was one of those kids who did everything well. She was the editor of the school newspaper, president of the student body, captain of the debate team, first violin, and an academic all-star with a 4.0 average. She would graduate in two months with a full-tuition scholarship to a top university.

She seemed to have a good family. Her father was a deputy sheriff, and her mother was the head nurse at a large hospital. They were active in the community and seemed to be supportive of all Therese's activities. One or both parents were at almost every debate tournament and concert. They seemed to love her and always encouraged her and praised her achievements.

Then, one day Therese took her dad's car, robbed a grocery store, and shot the clerk. The police arrested her three days later when they found her working as a dancer in a topless bar. It just didn't make sense. How could it have happened? Here's her story!

Therese's parent were hard-working and intelligent people. In public they appeared to be a happy couple. But over the years they had had a relationship of conflict. Thereases hated it when they fought.

It was always the same. Her mother was addicted to

downers. Each month she would do something illegal to get more drugs, and her father always got involved in helping her cover up her crimes. When she forged a prescription, he broke into the pharmacy and stole the faked doctor's order.

That night he was so angry that he hit her. As it happened, Therese had just come home from a debate tournament. She opened the door to find her mother sprawled on the floor with a bloody lip and her father standing over her, red-faced and fists doubled.

"Look," shouted Therese, "We won! Isn't that the biggest trophy you ever saw?"

"Yes," said her father, "It's great!"

"We're so proud of you," said her mother, getting up. "I slipped on that darn rug. Isn't that silly!"

Therese was responding by trying to be as perfect as possible. She viewed every A as a possible fight stopper. Each new achievement might save her mother from a beating. And often, it did. Her parents would get so involved in her successes that they would forget about their fight. Of course, Therese had no idea what they fought about.

Her father had always dreamed of being the Sheriff of Dune County, an elective position. The current sheriff was close to retirement, and he was next in line. He had a good record. Then it happened.

He discovered that his wife had been taking pain pills from the hospital's narcotic supply and replacing them with phonies. He knew that this story, once leaked, would forever ruin his chances of being elected sheriff.

So, once more, he decided to help her cover her crime. One night he slipped into the hospital, opened the supply rooms, shorted an electric socket, and started a fire. It should have worked, but a janitor happened along and put out the fire.

To make it worse, the fire chief told the sheriff that the fire appeared to have been arson. The sheriff ordered her father to nose around to see what he could find out. He did, and submitted a report that avoided the drug issue. But he was afraid the sheriff was suspicious. In fact, he was downright worried.

The fights between him and his wife became terrible. Finally, he beat her so badly that she could not go to work. Therese had been two blocks from home when she saw her father's police cruiser go by at high speed. Rushing home, she found her mother in the bathroom crying and trying to clean herself up.

"Mother, what is going on here?" she begged.

And her mother sobbed out the whole sad tale. "Your father said he couldn't live like this. He is going to turn himself in. But frankly, I'm worried that he may kill himself!"

"Oh, my gosh!" screamed Therese, "we've got to stop him." She ran to the phone and called the police dispatcher. "Tell my father that I've taken the car," she said. Then she started the car and drove to a convenience store. Running inside, she waved one of her father's pistols and shouted, "This is a stickup! Put all the money in a bag." The frightened clerk stuffed money into the bag as fast as he could. When he handed it to her, she shot him, jumped into the car, and sped away. Three days later, someone spotted her dancing at the club.

When she was arrested, she confessed to everything, including stealing narcotics from the hospital. But the sheriff didn't buy it. He went straight to her father and said, "We can do this the easy way or the hard way.

What's your pleasure?" With that, her father broke down and confessed everything.

Although heroes and rebels seem to be exact opposites, they are really very much alike. Both are trying to take the stress off a parent's drug-abusing behavior, and the resulting family problems, by putting the focus on themselves. In fact, when there is only one kid in a family, he or she may first try something heroic and if that doesn't work, try to get into trouble. Some kids switch back and forth most of their lives.

Clown—Serious One Relationships

The relationship between the clown and the serious one would be funny if it weren't so painful. The serious one in the family is often depressed. He or she has little confidence in the world or the future. It is as if life itself is too filled with danger to be taken lightly. The doors have to be locked, and so do the windows; the dog has to be fed, and so does the cat; breakfast has to be cooked, and so does dinner; the car has to be filled with gas every night, and the lawn mower should be filled up for next summer, just in case.

The clown helps lighten things up in the family. Why worry about tomorrow when you can tell a joke or play a joke on someone today? The world is friendly, and nothing bad is going to happen. Leave the dishes in the sink; we'll wash them tomorrow. We can cook breakfast anytime, and dinner isn't for hours. We can put gas in the car in the morning, and that lawn mower may not work by next summer. Let's have fun! We could put Handiwrap over Granny's glass of juice. With her eyesight, she'll never be able to see it.

Case Study: As she drove along, Gary's mother was annoyed. How could he have done such a thing? And at this time of night! Thinking about it made her head hurt. Mrs. Johnson was her oldest friend.

It all started when Mrs. Johnson had telephoned to say that her daughter, Amanda, had no date for the prom, and did she think that Gary might take her? She had been careful to make no commitment until she had spoken to Gary. But when he had agreed, the date was set. After all, Amanda was a very pretty girl.

Gary had rented a tuxedo, bought Amanda a corsage, borrowed the good car, and gone to pick up Amanda. That was hours ago. Everything seemed well with the world, so she had gone to sleep. Then the ringing phone awakened her. "Hello?" she said.

"This is Amanda," the voice said. "I hate to bother you, but Gary and I stopped for breakfast in Millerville on the way home. Gary said he was going for a newspaper, and I haven't seen him since. That was an hour ago. I'm worried that something has happened to him!"

"I'll be right there," she said looking at the clock. 3:30 a.m. How dare he? she thought. This was one of his favorite games. And where was her husband? All the bars close at 2:00, don't they? But never mind that, I've got to get Amanda.

Now, driving along the road to Millerville, she worried, What if it wasn't a joke? What if something had happened? Maybe someone had stabbed him? Shot him? Kidnapped him? Maybe he drove somewhere to get a paper. He could have had an accident. Amanda didn't say if the car was where they had left it! Oh, no! I forgot to ask from which restaurant Amanda called.

Just then, she saw their car sitting on the shoulder of the road. She hit the brakes, made a quick U-turn, and stopped right behind it. It seemed empty. She stepped out and walked over to the car. The motor was still running. As she got closer, she could see a note written in white shoe polish on the window. Squinting, she could read the words, "Where would you be now, if you weren't here?" Suddenly, she was aware of two faces looking at her through the window. It was Gary and Amanda. "Got ya!" shouted Gary.

"I'm sorry," yelled Amanda. "He waited till I called you, then he came and got me. I tried to call you back, but you were already gone!" Then Gary stepped on the gas and the engine roared and the tires squealed. They were gone!

"I'll kill you for this," shouted his mother. "You'll be grounded till you're thirty-five. You irresponsible . . . ," her words trailed off as she realized that she was standing there all alone in her night clothes shouting at no one who could hear.

By the time she got home, Gary had already left. There was a note on the refrigerator door: "Dad and I have gone fishing. See you tonight. Love, Gary. P.S. Thanks for getting me the date with Amanda. She was great!"

The relationship between the clown and the serious one can be hard to understand, especially if the serious one is a parent. This often happens when there is only one child. In this case, Gary's clowning covered up his father's drunken escapades. Mother had to be serious. She was single-handedly holding the family together.

Computer—Hysteric Relationships

Computer-hysteric relationships are common. Like the other relationships, each member has something the other needs. Computers are persons who react on the basis of thought instead of feelings. They don't like to feel, because they know that feelings are painful. Often, they have been the victims of abuse. Sometimes they were taught that "men aren't supposed to feel." In their family, that's how it was. Dad didn't feel, and neither did Granddad. Feelings were for women.

Hysterics are persons who react on the basis of feelings. They don't like thinking, because it usually gets them in trouble. They may have been criticized for thinking when they were children, or they may have learned that "women aren't supposed to think. It's a man's job." At least, it was in their families. Mom didn't think and neither did Grandma. Neither one of them could balance a checkbook.

Of course, sometimes the computer is a female and the hysteric is a male. It doesn't make much difference. The problem is that each person is locked into only one role.

Case Study: Margie didn't see anything wrong. So what if she had failed math again? She just didn't get it. Why did Mr. Sears make such a big deal out of it? She was standing in front of his desk, listening—well, maybe only half listening—to his lecture. "Margie," he said very loudly, "are you listening to me?"

"You don't like me, do you, Mr. Sears?"

"Liking has nothing to do with it, Margie," said Mr. Sears. "You failed math for the second time. You're a smart girl. I don't understand. Math is a very important subject. How will you ever balance your checkbook or make a budget?"

"Now you're mad at me," said Margie. "I knew you didn't like me!" She started to cry.

Mr. Sears looked at her and began to shout, "If you're going to be a crybaby, get out of my office to do it!"

Margie looked up at him and held her breath, making her face turn beet-red. Then suddenly she began sobbing hysterically, "You hate me. You hate me! You said you didn't, but you hate me!" With that she turned and ran into the hall.

The principal, Mrs. Jones, was passing the door as Margie emerged, still shrieking, "You hate me." Concerned, she went into Mr. Sears's office. "What's that about?" she asked.

"Margie keeps failing math," he said. "And she thinks it's because I hate her. The problem is, she doesn't do her homework."

Mrs. Jones said, "Let's ask her parents to come over for a conference. Maybe they can shed some light on this."

Two days later, Margie's parents, Mr. Sears, and Mrs. Jones were seated at the school conference table. After explaining what had happened, Mrs. Jones asked Margie's parents if they had anything to say. Margie's father said, "She's just like her mother—takes everything personally."

"Now just a minute," said her mother. "Flunking her once was bad enough. But what about her feelings? Don't you care how that must have made her feel?"

"Feelings!" shouted her father. "Who cares how she felt? There's more to life than feelings. Let's deal with the real issue. She failed and . . ."

"That's the trouble with you!" said her mother. "No one cares about her. No wonder she feels like you hate her. You can't expect her to pass math. I failed it myself, and so did my mother. She's not a man, you know."

"Whoa, hold it," said Mrs. Jones. "Do you hear what you're saying? If *you* don't believe in Margie, how will she ever believe in herself? Women can do math. In fact, they're some of the best mathematicians in the world. I'm going to put Margie in Mrs. Simm's summer class. I think she'll do better when she sees that a female can be very good at math."

That summer, Margie passed math with a B.

What Mrs. Jones didn't understand was that both Margie and her mother were hysterics, and her father and Mr. Sears were computers. They were simply acting out the roles they had all learned in their families.

Psychosomatic—Rigid One Relationships

This relationship is among the most damaging of all. People who are excessively rigid apply the same solution to every problem. When it doesn't work, they don't try a different solution. They just get angry and try harder.

This makes life extremely stressful—so stressful that some children have actually died because of it. Anyone living in this kind of a relationship needs to receive family counseling.

Case Study: This relationship has been the subject of an important scientific experiment by Salvador Minuchin, M.D., a highly regarded family therapist. Several years ago, he undertook an experiment at the Philadelphia Child Guidance Clinic.

Dr. Minuchin had been treating children who had mild diabetes. These children should have had very few problems with the disease, but they kept getting so sick that they had to be hospitalized. The experiment went like this:

Each child sat with Dr. Minuchin in an observation room with a one-way window through which they could see into another room. The people in the other room could not look back, however, because on their side the window was a mirror.

Dr. Minuchin put the child's family n the other room and gave them a problem to solve. It seemed easy, but it was impossible to do unless the family thought in a different way. As the child and the doctor watched, the family tried to solve the problem but became increasingly upset and frustrated. Finally, they began to fight. When that happened, the child's diabetes symptoms became worse. Dr. Minuchin concluded that it was the stress of the family's fighting that made the child sick. He also noticed that at least one family member absolutely refused to think in different ways. He called that person the "rigid one."

After many such experiments, Dr. Minuchin discovered that whenever a family included a member who was rigid, someone in the family was physically ill. Usually the illnesses were ulcers, headaches, backaches, asthma, stomachaches, or anorexia (an eating disorder in which the person tries to starve himself). He called the ailing family members the "psychosomatics." This word comes from two other words: *psycho*, meaning "thought," and *soma*, meaning "the body." Put together, they mean that the way a person thinks affects how that person feels. A psychosomatic is a person who handles the stress of living with a rigid person by becoming sick.

Note: Don't get the idea that psychosomatics are not really sick. Some die from their illness. The word merely describes how the person got sick.

Case Study: "Where do you think you're going dressed like that?" shouted Camille's mother.

"I was going to school," replied Camille.

"Not in this life," said her mother. "No child of mine is wearing blue jeans to school. You go to your room and put on something presentable. Now."

"But, Mom," stammered Camille. "All my friends wear blue jeans to school. I'll be the only one there in a dress."

"I don't care if your friends go to school in their underwear, you will go to school in a dress. That's how all decent children dress."

"Mom, please stop calling me a child," cried Camille. "I'm fourteen. You want everything to stay the same. But things change. My friends' parents let them wear makeup."

"Makeup! Makeup!" screamed her mother. "That does it! You're grounded for the rest of the semester. The very idea! Makeup at your age! At the rate you're going, you'll be pregnant by your next birthday!"

"Mother!" shouted Camille.

Then her mother went ballistic, screaming and cursing. "You slut! You're just like that worthless father of yours! You'll never amount to anything! All you ever think about is sex! And boys! You'll probably turn out to be a drunken slob—just like him!"

Camille could see it was useless. She didn't even try to say that this wasn't about sex; it was about wanting to fit in. She hung her head and went to her room. She had just taken off her jeans and was looking for a dress when the pain hit her as if a hot coal had dropped in her stomach. "Oh, no!" she cried. "Not again." She slipped the dress on and ran for the bus. By the time she got to school, she had started throwing up. A week later, the family doctor told her mother that Camille needed counseling. "No one her age should have such a problem with ulcers," he said.

"She's always thinking about boys and sex," said her mother.

The doctor had a strange expression on his face as he looked her mother right in the eye. "You need to go with her!" he said. "If you don't, I'm reporting you for child abuse!"

"You've got to be kidding!"

"Try me!" he said. "If you don't take some of the pressure off this kid, you'll either kill her or make her become obsessed with sex. Either way, that's abusive. It's your choice. Which will it be, family counseling or Child Protective Services?"

"All right," said her mother. "We'll all go!"

Camille was not like her father, but that made no difference. To her mother, everyone was the same—just no good: They thought wrong, they dressed wrong, and they acted wrong. And it was all about sex. Actually, Camille was put off by the idea of sex. She knew that her father's lack of responsibility in sexual matters had severely damaged her family.

In family counseling, her mother slowly came to know Camille as a person separate from her father. She also learned to deal with the pain of having her husband leave her for another woman. Things are very different between mother and daughter now. For her birthday, Camille's mother bought her a makeup tray. When Camille opened the package, she burst into tears of happiness. The card read, "You are a gift from God. I love you just as you are."

Mascot—Lost Child Relationships

The family mascot is a person who has learned to distract the family from its pain by being cute. A mascot is almost always the center of attention. He or she may be very talented and creative, but those gifts are not used primarily for self-fulfillment.

The lost child is the person who can't find a way to compete with the mascot. This person deals with pain by withdrawing from all relationships, both within and outside of the family.

Case Study: As babies, the Watson twins looked alike, smiled alike, cried alike, even threw fits alike. As they grew older, however, things began to change. Bell became more and more the center of attention, and Bill drew back. In fact, it sometimes seemed that the more popular Bell became, the less popular Bill was.

It wasn't that Bill didn't try; it was just that no one seemed to think he mattered. When Bell did something good, it was fantastic. When Bill did something good, no one noticed. In fact, no one noticed even when Bill did something bad.

"Honey, let's go out for lunch," said Jeff Watson one day. "We could stop off for a couple of beers on the way."

"What about your job?" asked his wife. "Don't you have to go back to work?"

"It's no big deal, Bonnie," said Jeff. "We're almost caught up. The boss will probably be glad to be rid of me for a while."

"Well, okay, but I hope you're right."

"Hey, baby," he said. "It's no big deal."

Within minutes Jeff had driven them to his favorite tavern, The Brass Bull. "Are you all right with this place?" he asked. She nodded, and they went inside. "Hey, Jack," he said to the bartender, "give us a couple of beers."

Three hours later, Bonnie was worried. "The kids will be home soon, Jeff. I need to be there. Please take me home."

"Okay," he said, "I need to get back to work, too." As they headed for the door, the bartender called, "Hey, Jeff, I got a call for you."

Jeff took the phone and said "Hello?" Then there was a long silence, followed by "Bonnie had a problem . . . She needed to talk to me . . . But, Mr. Keller, I was just . . . You don't understand . . . I wasn't just goofing off, I . . . Yes, sir. I understand."

Bonnie said, "What's the matter, Jeff?"

"He said I was fired, honey," Jeff answered. "Said I was a drunk, an alcoholic, that I needed help!"

Bonnie drove them home in silence. Bill and Bell had just reached the door when they pulled into the driveway.

"What's up?" asked Bell, noticing the worried look on her mother's face. When she got no answer, Bell said, "Hey, I made the cheerleading squad. Want to see my yells?" Soon she was jumping all over the driveway and shouting.

"Look at that girl go!" said her mother. "No wonder they chose you. You're great!" The cheers lasted until it was too dark to see. No one noticed that Bill had gone to his room and never returned.

Sharon Wegscheider-Cruse, the family-role expert who first described this role, believes that the lost child has the most severe problems in the family: A lost child doesn't identify with anyone.

Switchboard—Clam Relationships

The family switchboard is the person through whom most of the communication goes. This is especially true when tension is high in the family.

The family clam responds to stress by "clamming up" around the rest of the family about the stressful issue. Because of the "specialness" of their relationship, the clam will talk only to the switchboard, who must then relay the message to the others.

Case Study: Melissa's parents were both teachers at the Haught Junior High School. Melissa dropped then off each day on her way to Paskel High and picked them up on her way home.

One day when she pulled up to the front of Haught, they got into the car without saying a word. This might have surprised some people, but Melissa was used to it. She would find out what the problem was later. So she just turned up the radio and drove on without saying a word.

At home, she went to her room to do her homework. Her parents sat on the couch and watched television—still without anyone having said a word.

After a few minutes her father went to Melissa's room, sat down on the bed, and said, "I think your mother is upset about something. Would you see if you can find out what it is?"

"Sure, Dad," said Melissa. She went downstairs and sat beside her mother. "Dad thinks you're angry with him. Are you?"

"No, honey. Tell your dad that I saw that lady he dated when we were separated. I'm not mad at him, but it still hurts when I see her."

"Okay, Mom," Melissa said. "I'll tell him." Then she went back to her father and said, "Mom's not mad at you. She ran into that lady that you dated when the two of you were separated that time ten years ago. She says it still hurts. That's all."

"Thanks, honey!" he said, "I'm glad it was nothing serious."

"Me, too!" said Melissa.

Her father gave her a quick hug, when downstairs, sat down by his wife, and started watching television again.

It is worth noting that one of the problems in switchboard-clam relationships is difficulty talking about feelings. Because of this, they communicate in a circle—to someone who is not involved in the problem. That, of course, means that they will never be able to solve the problem.

The case studies in this chapter all came from families in which one or both of the parents were alcoholic or drug-addicted. It is extremely painful to live in these families. The relationships illustrated here are the result of that family pain.

> *Note:* The family roles discussed here were first discovered and described by these experts: Virginia Satir (Computer, Placator—also called Peacemaker and Martyr); Sharon Wegscheider-Cruse (Mascot, Rebel, Hero, and Lost Child); Salvador Minuchin (Psychosomatic, Rigid One); Evelyn Leite (Clown); Claudia Black (Responsible One—also called the Parentified Child); and myself—Lawrence Clayton (Turtle, Grand Inquisitor, Hysteric, Switchboard, Clam, Serious One, Warrior, Incompetent One).

CHAPTER 10

The Eldest Child of A Drug-Abusing Parent

There is another role you may have to play, especially if you are the oldest in the family. That role is "parent" to younger brothers and sisters, particularly if your parents are not functioning in their roles.

You may be the one who has to impose rules on younger kids or take them places, see that they keep their dentist appointments, keep them from pigging on junk food, break up fights.

Much of the time that is not a particularly rewarding experience. The younger kids resent you and are likely to say, "You aren't my boss!"

It may be tempting sometimes to be too hard on them—maybe you can't control your parents, but by gosh you can control the state of your little brother's room or what little sister spends her allowance on. The kids are right when they say you are being a tyrant.

You may also take it hard when they have problems. It can seem like your fault that your little brother got into a fight in school and is now in the principal's office.

Your parents can react in a number of ways to your trying to take over their job. They may resent it, seeing themselves as perfectly capable of handling it. They may happily push the role off on you—it gets them out from under the responsibility. Or they may not even be aware that you are trying in some ways to fill their shoes.

Sometimes they have all those reactions, which confuses everybody.

If you are acting as the parent, realize that you can't really take over the role and that there are limits to what you can do. You are, after all, basically still a kid.

Be reasonable with young brothers and sisters. Exercising authority just to exercise authority is never a good decision, even if it makes you feel good right then. It's too easy to slip into being an obnoxious jerk and breed resentment in them.

Try to be consistent. Uncertainty is already a big factor in everyone's life. Don't add to it if you can help it.

If you are a younger member of the family and an older brother or sister is trying to act as Mom or Dad or both, try not to make things harder. Your brother or sister has taken on a difficult role (or had it pushed off on him or her) and may not enjoy it one whit more than you enjoy having him or her tell you what to do.

Try to cooperate with each other and get along as well as you can. You are in a very difficult situation. Conflict between yourselves will just make it worse.

Case Study: Kinley is sixteen, Matthew is twelve, and Raven is nine. Their parents are divorced; their mother is an alcoholic. Her first act when she comes home from work is to reach for a bottle. She has usually passed out by 8 o'clock.

Kinley is the one who makes Matt and Raven do their homework and sees that they have clothes ready for school the next day.

Now and then Mom comes out of her alcoholic stupor and becomes "Supermom." She cleans the house to a shine, waxes floors, bakes cookies, takes the kids to the park or the zoo on weekends. And she sometimes shows her resentment at Kinley's taking over her role. Unfortunately, those times don't last. Before long she is drinking again.

Matt and Raven also resent Kinley's acting as Mom. In fact, Kinley feels, Matt sometimes goes out of his way to be obnoxious. One day when Matt had flatly refused to clean his room (Kinley had walked in and said, "Were there any survivors of whatever happened here?"), he and Kinley wound up in a shouting match, with Raven joining in that she was *not* going to do her homework tonight.

"You're not my boss!" Raven howled.

"All right," Kinley said quietly, "You don't like my trying to hold things together around here. I've been thinking for quite a while about going to live with Dad. You want to be on your own—maybe that would be better for everyone."

Once Matt and Raven had a chance to think it over, they realized that it wouldn't be better. Kinley cooked most of their meals, saw that they had something to wear to school that looked good, made sure they had lunch money—things Mom couldn't be trusted to do.

The three sat down and talked out some of their differences. Kinley realized that she had been harder on them than was probably necessary, and she agreed to ease up on some of the rules and regulations.

All three agreed that they had enough to cope with handling Mom's problem without being at each other's throats as well.

CHAPTER 11

How Your Parent's Drug Abuse Affects You

Teenagers who grow up in a home where one or both parents are addicted to drugs or alcohol often think they are the only ones who feel the way they do. That is not true.

Experts agree that all children of addicted parents have problems in most of the following areas. Of course, not every person who grows up in an alcoholic home will have all of these problems. But they will have at least six of them.

1. They tend to isolate themselves, and they are frightened of authority figures (Robert Subby).

One of the reasons this is true is because children of addicts have discovered that people in authority frequently abuse their power. They have no way of knowing which ones will and which ones won't.

Case Study: Gary had always felt guilty about his dad's drinking. In fact, he sometimes thought he was responsible for it. He tried hard to get better grades, to make Dad proud, not to anger him. But nothing he did made any difference.

Gary also had a terrific crush on Eileen, although he never got up the nerve even to speak to her. One day when he came home he found Eileen helping his mother as part of a "Maid for a Club" school project. When he walked in, Eileen was in the kitchen ironing shirts. Mom winked at him—she knew how he felt about Eileen. When Eileen had finished her chores Mom said, "Honey, why don't you drive Eileen home?"

Gary's heart jumped. He would finally get a real chance to talk to Eileen.

There was only one problem: Dad had the keys to the car, and he was in the den drunk as usual. When Gary asked for the keys, Dad bellowed, "What the #¢$% do you want the @#¢$%@ keys for, anyway?"

Gary cringed and said in a small voice, "To take Eileen home."

Dad fished in his pocket for the keys and tossed them to Gary, saying, "Just don't get her pregnant!"

Gary died a thousand deaths as he took the keys. He glanced at Eileen—her face was fiery red. Not a word was exchanged between Gary and Eileen as they drove. Gary knew he would never have the nerve to speak to her again. He would also be sure that nobody invited kids to his house again.

These children have had thousands of similar experiences. For them it's often safer to be alone.

2. They tend to be approval seekers and have little sense of their own identity (Janet Woititz).

Children of alcoholics desperately want acceptance, something they may never have received at home. They will change themselves to whatever anyone wants them to be in hope of being accepted.

Case Study: Linda and her sister Joanne saved their money for a pumpkin for Halloween. When they got it home, they asked Mom to carve it for them. The only problem was that Mom was "that way" again.

She cut the top off the pumpkin, then scooped out handfuls of the insides and threw them on the floor, screaming, "You wanted this damned pumpkin, you clean up the mess."

Because they were afraid of Mom's anger, they did as they were told. They even acted happy that Mom was "letting" them help. Later, when Mom slipped cutting the mouth and ruined the pumpkin, they acted as if it didn't matter.

Children of addicts lose any sense of who they are and what they feel. They seek approval from others, never realizing that they are sacrificing something very precious: their own sense of identity.

3. They are frightened by anger and criticism (Claudia Black).

These are children who have discovered that anger is dangerous. They may have seen their mothers, sisters, and brothers beaten. And they, themselves, may have been beaten.

Case Study: Keith Jr. was so proud of himself: He had bought his father an ice cream cone. Not just any ice cream cone, but Big Keith's favorite, Rocky Road. And not only Rocky Road, but a double scoop!

He imagined how happy Dad would be. But when he actually handed the ice cream to Big Keith, not a word was spoken. Big Keith started to eat it, but his hands were unsteady and the top scoop fell off and landed in his lap. He started to swear furiously and yelled, "What is wrong with you? You know I hate sticky stuff on me! Can't you do anything right?" Then Big Keith began to hit him.

Children of alcoholics or addicts never know when criticism and anger will lead to abuse—emotional, physical, sexual, or all three.

4. They feel guilty when they stand up for themselves (George Vaillant).

These teenagers truly believe that they are unworthy. Emotional abuse has always been a part of their lives.

Case Study: Debbie's alcoholic mother created a world of rules—you must do this, you must never say that—and if Debbie inadvertently broke a rule her mother was furious. Debbie's acceptance was always based on performance. Over and over she had heard, "You're nothing but trash. You'll never amount to anything."

One day the home ec teacher came in and found everyone in Debbie's kitchen throwing muffins at each other. All except Debbie, who was standing quietly to one side. The teacher slapped a detention on everyone, until Debbie said, "But I didn't do anything," and the others agreed that she hadn't.

Later Debbie felt terribly guilty, as if she should have

been in detention, too. In fact, she waited after school until her friends got out of detention and walked home with them.

These teenagers truly believe that they are unworthy. Emotional abuse has always been part of their lives.

5. They develop either underresponsibility or overresponsibility (Janet Woititz).

Kids who have been blamed for everything in an addicted parent's life either become addicted to trying to "fix" everything, or they become helpless.

Case Study: Cindy opened the bathroom door to find her father mainlining heroin, holding a needle, a cord tied around his arm. He screamed at her, "What do you expect? You and that mother of yours! I wouldn't need to do this if it weren't for you!"

After that Cindy felt as if it was her fault every time Dad didn't come home. She felt responsible when her little sisters were hungry or she heard Mom crying late at night. She found herself doing things like collecting and selling empty pop bottles so her sisters could eat. When Dad was really wiped out, she hid his car keys so he couldn't drive. In fact, she seemed more like a parent than he did.

Billy responded differently to the stress in his family. He also believed that his dad's drug use was his fault, but he had given up long ago.

Dad constantly said things like, "You screw up everything you touch. You're accident-prone. Oh, God, don't let Billy fix it."

When Billy's little sister was hungry, Billy cried. When Dad came home angry, Billy hid until Dad was asleep.

Children of drug-abusing parents tend to grow up too quickly or too slowly. They have to behave like adults or like infants. They are either fifteen going on fifty, or fifteen going on two. They are never fifteen going on sixteen, because they seldom get to act or feel their real age.

6. Children of addicts tend to look for "victims" to help (Robert Subby).

These kids often identify with the underdog, because they are victims, too. They have been robbed of their childhood. They feel sorry for others because it would be too painful to feel sorry for themselves.

Case Study: Janice liked to pick up and find homes for stray dogs because she was sure they would get run over if she didn't help them.

She also wanted to help little Jamie who lived in the apartment below her. The other kids seemed to pick on Jamie.

One day several of them were making fun of Jamie. Janice stepped in and told them to leave him alone. One of the kids grabbed Janice's earring and ripped it off, cutting her ear.

The next day Jamie told Janice to leave her alone.

That evening Dad noticed that Janice was upset. He began to ridicule her, saying, "Oh, look at the crybaby! Aren't you a little old for that?"

No one ever helped Janice.

When children of addicts find a victim to help, they try to give that person what they themselves desperately want—love enough to make them feel safe.

7. They become addicted to excitement and chaos (Ellen Morehouse).

Adolescents growing up in severely disturbed homes live in a cycle. Graphically, it looks like this:

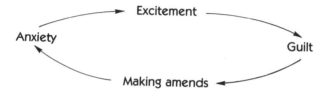

Excitement takes many forms in the family with an addicted parent. A child never knows when a parent will come home, whether the parent will be straight or loaded, kind or abusive. When the crisis occurs the family all draws together. Dad may even take charge, and everybody does his part to overcome the problem.

Case Study: Larry came home to find yet another electricity cutoff notice on the door. He could feel his heart pounding as he rushed into the house and to the telepone. Mom really sounded concerned and was home in minutes. She took charge, sending Larry to Uncle John's store for a loan. Roy went to Aunt Phyllis's house, and Rick called Dad, getting him only after an argument with their stepmother. But everyone helped, and by evening the electricity was on again. As the utility truck pulled away,

Mom said, "Larry, if you didn't leave the lights on all day, I could pay this bill myself."

All of the adults looked at Larry. He felt terrible—it was all his fault. The next morning he got up early, cooked breakfast for his brothers and his Mom, and washed the dishes. When he got home from school, he cooked dinner and tried to get his homework done.

Trying to get the potatoes done at the same time as the peas was hard. Trying to concentrate on his homework while trying to get the peas and potatoes done made him very nervous.

And Mom didn't come home that night.

Was she just drunk, or had she been in an accident? Wondering and worrying about it, Larry stayed awake until after midnight. Mom still wasn't home when they went to school the next morning. Larry couldn't even think that day.

That night she came home right after work as though nothing had happened. Nobody mentioned her not being home the night before.

When Larry got home from school the next day there was a letter from the landlord: "Your rent is past due. If not paid immediately, you will have to vacate your apartment." Larry ran for the telephone. His heart was beating wildly.

Children growing up with an addicted parent become addicted to a chaotic style of life. They begin to see it as normal. The only time they feel good about themselves is during a crisis.

8. They confuse love with pity (Claudia Black).

These children have never experienced real love, never

had a chance to give love or feel love for themselves. They have learned only to feel sorry for themselves.

Case Study: Phillip's parents were both alcoholic. He was uncertain what to do around them most of the time. They fought constantly, calling each other horrible names. When his mother really got onto Dad, Phillip had "warm feelings" for him. He thought that was love.

If his mother said enough hateful things, his father would explode and beat her viciously. Afterward Phillip would wipe the blood from her face, all the while crying and saying, "I love you, Mom," over and over.

Phillip felt sorry for his mother, but he didn't love her. He had never known what love was because no one had ever loved him. Addicted people always put their addiction before other people.

When Phillip began dating, he found someone he could feel sorry for. Betty Lou's mother was terribly abusive to her. There had been times when she tied Betty Jo to a post in the basement and beat her unconscious. Phillip often held Betty Lou for hours, telling her of his love and saying that he would marry her and take her away to a safe place.

Pity can be a very strong emotion. When a child of an addict encounters someone for whom she feels pity, there is an instant identification. As this emotion overwhelms the child, she believes it is love.

9. They usually don't know what they feel (Barbara Naiditch).

Children who grow up in homes where one of the parents is addicted tend to distance themselves from their feelings. They have learned to protect themselves by denying what they feel.

Case Study: Greg was feeling closer all the time to his new stepbrother. This was the first time they had gone to the movies together. Now Greg tried to give John a hug. He had always given Dad a hug. But now he felt his stepbrother stiffen and pull away.

John said, "What are you, a queer or something?"

Greg didn't know what a queer was, but he knew it wasn't good. He felt hurt, and tears came to his eyes.

John said, "What's wrong with you now? You're just a big sissy."

Greg couldn't know that living with an alcoholic father most of his life had made John the way he was, that feelings were unacceptable to him, that to acknowledge feelings opened him up to ridicule.

Feeling are dangerous for a child of an addict. With them comes vulnerability, and that is not good in the presence of an addicted parent. The only outcome is more pain.

10. They judge themselves harshly and have low self-esteem (Janet Woititz).

Children of addicts are only applying what they have learned—to be angry and harsh in their judgment of themselves. It is how they have been treated by the most powerful people in their lives—their parents.

Case Study: Charley had wanted to be a writer all her life, something that her drug-using parents found hilarious. One day at school the teacher announced an essay contest for tenth-graders. The first prize was $500, which to Charley sounded like a fortune.

She wrote her essay and rewrote it, but as the deadline approached she began to feel more and more that it was "just a lot of silly kid stuff." She didn't bother to send it in.

Two days later the English teacher stopped her after class and handed her her essay; it had been turned in accidentally with a homework assignment.

"Charley, why on earth didn't you submit this? It is excellent."

Charley just shuffled her feet and mumbled, "I thought it was too dumb. My folks say the stuff I write is usually dumb."

"Charley, I was one of the judges in that contest. This is much better than the paper that won."

How can any child learn to love without having first been loved? It is an almost impossible task.

11. They overcompensate by acting superior (Robert Subby).

Acting superior is one of the primary defenses against the pain of living in an alcoholic family. These kids are often afraid to let anyone get close to them. They put on an "I'm too good for you" act to protect themselves from getting close to others. They know that can be painful.

Don't confuse these kids' actions with reality.

They may secretly want to have a close relationship. They just don't believe they can have one in which they do not get hurt.

Case Study: Peter knew that his father wouldn't be coming home that night. After all, it was payday. It didn't matter that Peter's jeans had holes in them and were too short now. By the time Dad got home all the money would be gone.

Peter liked Roberta, but that morning he had seen her looking at his ankles, all too visible now. But that evening Roberta walked up to him and handed him an envelope. He opened it and read, "Roberta Thomas requests your presence at a birthday party given in her honor . . . " He didn't read the rest of it. He knew he couldn't go to a party in his scruffy clothes, and he didn't have money for a present.

He sniffed and said, "I don't go to seventh-graders' stupid parties. They're so immature." Roberta's smile faded as Peter turned away and shouted, "Hey, Jack, look what this dumb chick handed me. Can you believe it?"

The two boys took off together, laughing. No one noticed how depressed Peter was for the next several weeks.

Children growing up in drug-abusing homes learn only a few coping mechanisms. Their parents are not the best role models from whom to learn healthy coping strategies. Acting superior may be perceived as less painful than the alternative: accepting the fact that their entire lives are painful.

12. They are terrified of being abandoned (Jane Middleton-Moz and Lorie Dwinell).

Children with drug-abusing parents have no opportunity to experiment with independence before it is thrust upon them. Consequently, they never really achieve it.

Case Study: One of the first things Carlos can remember is waking up in his father's car with his little brother, Juan, crying. It was cold, and he was hungry. He rubbed the sleep from his eyes and looked around.

There were a few other cars and a building with lights not far away. He could hear music and laughter coming from the building.

Then the door opened, and a man came out. He stumbled against the car, then saw Carlos and began to scream at him and beat his fists on the car window.

Carlos was terrified. The man continued to scream and beat on the window for a long time before he finally left. It was much longer before Carlos's father returned.

Carlos is seventeen now, and he still hates being alone. He sees himself as a helpless victim most of the time. His girlfriend, Julia, often leaves him to dance with other boys at the club where they hang out, and Carlos hates that. Once she left with Phil and didn't return for over an hour. A friend told Carlos that he had seen them making out in Phil's car. Furious, Carlos drove home alone. But in a couple of hours Julia called. She said she was sorry, would he come back to the club?

He would. He was on his way in minutes.

Julia has done this to him more than once, and he has always taken her back. Each time his self-image is a little lower and he behaves more dependently. Carlos is terrified that one day Julia won't come back.

Independence is a process. It happens a step at a time. These children are either pushed too fast or held too tightly. Either extreme is deadly.

13. They do not know what "normal" is (Janet Woititz).

These children grow up in homes that are not normal. The way their parents relate to each other and to them is not normal. Behavior in their families is not normal. In fact, very little of their experience in life is normal.

Case Study: Janette saw her stepfather's behavior as normal. It was how she had grown up. Every morning he would break two raw eggs in a large glass and fill the glass with whiskey. Janette thought that was normal.

She also thought that all her friends' fathers had sex with them—until one day she asked her best friend, Mitzi. Mitzi acted shocked and disgusted, and Janette felt that she had made a horrible mistake by asking. She felt betrayed by Mitzi. After all, they had talked about everything else. Now Mitzi acted as if this was a big deal. Well, it wasn't to Janette. After all, her stepfather had sex with both of her older sisters, and besides Mom was often so tired.

Maybe Mitzi just didn't want her as a friend any longer. Janette began screaming at Mitzi because she was such a traitor.

Children of drug-abusing parents have not had life experiences upon which to build a model for the concept of "normal." Sometimes they decide that normal is what their parents don't do, but that still leaves them with little understanding of what "normal" is.

14. They have difficulty completing projects (Janet Woititz)

Children of addicted parents do not receive consistent rewards for completing tasks. That leaves them feeling discouraged by life or about life.

Case Study: Ollina was very happy. Today she had gotten her first paycheck for her first real job. It was only picking up papers at the hamburger joint, but it was a job. Now she would be able to buy that pretty sweater. She was so tired of hand-me-downs. Her own new sweater! She couldn't remember the last new thing she had had to wear. She tore open the envelope with trembling fingers; inside was a green check for $36.52. Wow, she could even buy the matching mittens. When she got home she could hardly wait to show it to her mother.

Mom said, "Here, Ollina, I'll take it to the bank and cash it for you."

Suddenly Ollina was afraid. She knew that Mom would buy pot with it, just as she did with the child-support money. She said, "No, Mom, I'll cash it."

Her mother grabbed the check and put it in her pocket, saying, "You've got to go to school tomorrow. When you get home, I'll have your money."

Ollina doubted that very much, but she could not bring herself to say anything but, "OK, Mom."

The next day every class seemed two hours long. When school was finally out Ollina ran home, but before she got to the door she knew it was too late. Uncle Bill's car was in the driveway, and she could hear the guitar playing and her mother laughing. Ollina knew she was stoned.

She slowly opened the door. Through the haze, she could see Uncle Bill and Mom sitting on the couch, passing a joint back and forth. All her mother said was, "So what are you looking at? Get your clothes changed. You've got a job, you know."

That evening Ollina quit her job.

Children of drug-abusing parents are usually very discouraged people. They have not had a chance to learn that hard work and diligence are rewarded.

15. They lie when it would be just as easy to tell the truth (Janet Woititz).

The truth does not set the child of an addict free—it is painful. The truth is that they have at least one parent for whom booze is much more important than are the children. For them, it is better to learn to lie than to face this truth.

Case Study: Holly's mother was high again. Holly could tell that she was in a good mood. Mom said, "Honey, I think I'm going to get a good job for a change. I'll make lots of money, and we'll have the biggest Christmas ever!"

"I know," Holly said, "and you can get me that big doll with the blue eyes. You're the best mom a kid could ever have."

Holly knew that her mother never kept the promises she made when she was high. Still, it was fun to pretend. It was the only chance she got to have fun with her. When Mom was coming down off speed, she was depressed, hateful, and abusive, sometimes violently so. But this part was fun.

Christmas came and went, and there was no doll with blue eyes or any other presents. Back in school, Pam said, "Hey, Holly, what did you get for Christmas? I got a new sweater, Guess jeans, and a new doll."

Holly said, "I got a life-size doll with blue eyes and some new black Keds."

"Wear your Keds tomorrow, and I'll wear my Guess jeans."

Holly shook her head. "I gave my Keds to my cousin because she didn't get anything for Christmas."

"Wow, that was quite a sacrifice to make."

"Not really. Her dad's out of work, and I did get my doll."

"I'll come over after school and we can play dolls."

"No, you can't come over," Holly said quickly, "my mom's sick."

"Why don't you bring your doll and come over to my house?"

"I'll have to stay home and take care of Mom."

Kids with addicted parents find that lying is less painful than telling the truth. It eventually becomes a habit. So they lie even when telling the truth would be easier. Not only that, but they feel threatened and attacked when others ask questions.

16. They have trouble having fun (Janet Woititz).

What is fun about being in the home of an addict? The rages? The embarrassment? The lack of loving concern? How can play happen in this environment? The truth is, it doesn't. Oh, they may attempt to play, but they are always on guard.

Case Study: Jennifer and Jessie were playing cards. Jennifer laid down a Jack and Jessie laid down a Queen. Jessie said, "I win!"

"No, you don't," Jennifer insisted. "All face cards are worth ten points."

Jessie screamed, "Not in War. Mom, Jennifer's cheating again."

Their mother had just dozed off when she heard that. Now she was angry when she came into the den. "What's wrong with you girls? You know I hate fighting. I'll teach you to fight!" and she slapped both of them and grabbed the cards, ripping them in half one at time.

A week later Jennifer and Jessie were attending her funeral. Her suicide note said, "I never was any good as a mother. You will probably hate me for doing this. I never knew how to do anything right. Some people should just quit trying."

After the funeral Aunt Gladys said, "You will have to help your dad, now that your mom is gone." That surprised them because they had been doing Mom's job for years. So what else was new?

Kids with addicted parents are often overly mature. As if they missed adolescence, they seem to go from five to thirty-five years of age. That's because they often have to do what their parents don't do.

17. They take themselves too seriously (Janet Woititz).

Being the child of an addict is serious business. Sometimes even the necessities of life are forfeited if money is limited. Because of this, these children are very serious.

Case Study: After their mother's funeral, Jennifer and Jessie realized that their father was severely depressed. He stayed that way for the next eight months. That was when the girls went to his room and gave him a good talking-to. Jennifer said, "Dad, this is crazy. You've got a job, a house, a car, and us. It's time you went out and met a lady. That's what we want you to do."

Jessie said, "We've arranged to have Aunt Gladys stay with us so you can have some time out on your own."

The next week Jennifer tried out for the lead in the school play. She clearly had the best singing voice and she was cute, but the director said, "She's just too serious. This is a light, romantic comedy. She comes across like something from a Shakespearean tragedy."

Jennifer told him that he would regret his decision when she was a Hollywood movie star.

Jessie refused to go out for basketball that year, claiming that she had "more important responsibilities."

At times the whole family may depend on the child of an addict. While this is unfair, it sometimes means the survival of the family. Friends may be playing with dolls, but this child is wondering if her parent is still alive, has a job, or is in jail.

18. They have trouble establishing and maintaining intimate relationships (Janet Woititz).

Parents who use drugs repress almost all of their feelings except anger, and they insist that family members do likewise. They repress feelings because they feel so bad about themselves. If they were to get in touch with any of their feelings, they would get in touch with all of them— and they couldn't handle that.

The result is that kids with drug-abusing parents end up expressing only thoughts and repressing feelings. That makes it very hard to establish intimate relationships. On those rare occasions when they do form a relationship with a minor level of intimacy, they distance themselves whenever the other person wants to talk about feelings. That almost always results in the end of the relationship.

Case Study: Emil, almost twenty and a sophomore in college, was very depressed. He had begun to see signs, which he certainly recognized by now, that his girlfriend Patti was beginning to want out of the relationship. They had been dating for over a year, and lately he had begun to think that she was the girl he wanted to marry. But now Patti, like every other girl he had seriously dated, was beginning to be "busy" a lot of times when he called, seemed to go with girlfriends a lot of places that she used to go with him—oh, yes, he knew the signs well enough by now.

He could never have understood Patti's point of view. She liked him, too, liked him a lot. But whenever she wanted to talk about her feelings for him, and find out his feelings for her, suddenly it was as if he were in the next county. He more or less ignored what she was trying to communicate.

Since he could never discuss the subject of feelings, Patti could only conclude that Emil had no special feelings for her, despite the fact that he said he loved her. She would rather look for a guy who could express what he felt.

Feelings are an important part of our lives. About half of the human brain is designed to deal with feelings. These children are taught to use the half that is designed to think and to deny the feeling half—to use only half their brain.

19. They overreact to changes over which they have no control (Janet Woititz).

Children who grow up with addicted parents try to control as much of their environment as possible. When a change takes place that they cannot control, they experience it as extremely stressful and usually overreact to it.

Case Study: Paul was nine years old, from a family that was really messed up. When they were totally without money, Paul could usually manage to shoplift something that could be sold or pawned. He managed, somehow, to keep things under control.

One day he came home from school to find his mother and little brothers sitting on the sidewalk with their belongings. The building had been condemned, his mother told him.

Paul started crying and using dirty words. Things were out of control and he couldn't handle it.

But a shelter for homeless families took them in. The woman there was very kind and understanding. Everything seemed better.

A few days later Paul came home from school to discover that his family had been moved to other rooms. The woman in charge tried to explain that they needed to paint the first rooms the family had lived in. But Paul didn't listen; he was crying and swearing.

Controlling chaos increasingly becomes a way for dealing with the uncertainty of living with an addicted parent. These children often do not know the difference between good changes and bad changes. So they overreact to all change.

20. They believe they are different from other people (Janet Woititz).

Although that is true is some respects, these children believe they are different in more ways than they really are. The primary reason is that they feel different.

Case Study: Sherri was seventeen when her boyfriend told her that he felt "too tied down" and wanted to date other girls. Sherri had sort of expected it. Her father was always saying things like that to her mom. Sherri remembered the terrible fight her parents had had when she was only seven. She had waked up one night to hear her father shouting and her mother begging and crying, "Please don't leave! What about the children?"

"The hell with you and the hell with the kids. I'm going to move in with Jackie!" her father yelled.

So what else was new?

Her father had left several times, but he had always come back—at least until that last time.

Sherri was just like her mother. No boy would ever stay with her. But she wouldn't beg like her mother—no way was she ever going to do that!

"So to hell with you!" she shouted at her boyfriend, and suddenly realized how much like her father she sounded.

Children of addicted parents know only two roles in life—victim and victimizer. Both are painful. They are strangers to the healthy place between the two extremes that is called assertive, responsible behavior. To live and function in such a place, a teenager needs to feel a good deal of self-worth. These kids feel worthless and believe that they are no good.

21. They are extremely loyal, even when it is undeserved (Janet Woititz).

These children have spent most, if not all, of their lives in families where loyalty is demanded but seldom deserved. As they mature, this accustomed way of living is transferred to other relationships.

Case Study: Donna's mother was always on speed, either way up or way down. She was never emotionally available to Donna and her younger sister. Several times the social worker talked to Donna about her mother's drug use, but Donna always staunchly defended her, denying that anything was wrong.

Donna's English teacher was also her basketball coach. He often told off-color jokes in class and frequently swore during practice. And sometimes he seemed to be a little too free with his hands, once even fondling Donna's breasts. The one thing Mr. Johnson did do was to treat Donna "nicely"; that is, he talked kindly to her and didn't hit her. The principal called Donna to the office once to ask about the coach and whether he had done anything that seemed wrong to her.

"Oh, no!" Donna shook her head. "He's a great guy, the best coach in the world."

Children of addicts have had to defend their parents many times. Loyalty has become a habit. They often apply it even after they are grown men and women. This makes them vulnerable to all sorts of people. A spouse, a boss, or a minister can abuse their children or take their money. It makes little difference; they will loyally defend that person forever.

22. They are impulsive (Janet Woititz).

They learned to be impulsive, to live for the moment, from their parents. They have also learned to get whatever pleasure they can get, *now*. Tomorrow it could be gone forever.

Case Study: Gina's mother gave her twenty dollars to buy groceries on the way home from school. During lunch break she and her best friend, Donita, went to the school bookstore.

"Look, Gina, the new school sweatshirts are out," Donita said excitedly.

"They're beautiful, and only eight dollars," Gina said enthusiastically. She decided to buy one; after all, Mom did owe her ten dollars in allowance money.

Donita said, "My dad will buy me one, but they'll all be gone by the time he gets back from his business trip. Will you lend me the money, Gina?"

"Sure," Gina said, digging in her purse.

At home that night Gina told her mother that she had had no other choice. Donita wanted a sweatshirt, and they would all have been gone. Gina never considered that her mother might not have another twenty dollars. She never thought about putting the sweatshirts on layaway. She acted on impulse.

This happens because people in addicted families learn to live for the moment, to get what pleasure they can right now, before things change and the opportunity is gone forever.

23. They have difficulty identifying and expressing their feelings (Barbara Naiditch).

It is not okay to have feelings in alcoholic families. To be more precise, only the alcoholic parent may have feelings, and the only one he or she usually expresses is anger. To express feelings would risk opening the door to the agonizing pain in which they all live. So the whole family repress their feelings. Eventually they don't even know what they do feel.

Case Study: Mark wanted to try out for the basketball team, but he knew that Dad wanted him to work at the gas station after school, so he didn't show up. When the coach asked where he had been, he said, "Doing something useful."

The coach said, "But you told me you really wanted to try to make the team this year."

Mark shrugged and said, "I just changed my mind."

Two years later Mark's dog was run over right in front of him and his girlfriend Stephanie. Stephanie was terribly upset and crying, but Mark just took his dog's body to the backyard and buried it. Even so, he seemed depressed the next day. Stephanie asked what he was feeling. He replied, "I'm not really sure."

"Maybe you're upset about Spot."

Mark looked surprised. "I don't think so."

People who do therapy with children of addicts spend most of their time trying to undo the damage that has been done because of these children's having had to hide their feelings. Sometimes they are hidden so well that no one can find them.

24. They believe they have no choice about the way they live their lives (Claudia Black).

Kids in these families have been disappointed and discouraged all their lives. They think they just don't matter.

Case Study: James got a new bicycle for Christmas. It was the best bicycle he had ever seen. He couldn't believe it.

Mom had actually kept her promise. She had made a bargain with him: She would put $50 down on the bike if he would earn the other $22.50. He had mowed lawns, picked up cans, baby-sat, and washed Mrs. Green's windows.

Now he had the bicycle, and it was even the color he

wanted. He loved that bike. It was perfect. He rode it every single day for three weeks. Then one morning the bike was gone.

He looked everywhere, even reported it to the police, but it was hopeless. It was gone. Mom just said. "Maybe it will turn up," and she objected that he had called the cops. James hoped against hope that he would find it—at least, he hoped that until he overheard his mother telling his aunt, "The check bounced. I feel terrible, but I had to take it back."

James went to his room and cried and cried. "It's just like Dad's drinking," he thought. "I didn't have any control over that, either. I could never get him to stop. I wonder where he is now?"

"Hoping is for fools. Thinking things will ever get better is for idiots," James thought, as he drifted off to sleep.

Choice is learned, and these children don't learn it. It is important for children to win some of the arguments in their own home. Those who don't become easy targets for peer pressure. The child who doesn't have a vote in her own home won't have one in the back seat of a car. It makes no difference whether the issue is sex or drugs; they don't even know they have a vote.

25. They are controlling (Timmen Cermak).

Some children of addicts respond in the opposite direction from those in the preceding case study: They try to control everything in an attempt to have some order in their lives. This, of course, costs them a lot of friends.

Case Study: When Jerry answered the knock at the door, he was surprised to see two policemen standing on the porch.

"Can I help you?" he asked, nervously.

One of them said, "Does May Johnson live here?"

"Yes, she's my mother."

"Is your father home?"

"I haven't seen my dad in years. Look, what's wrong?"

"Well, your mother has been in an accident and she's been badly hurt, very badly. She's at Metropolitan Hospital."

The policemen called social services and placed Jerry and his sister in foster care. By the time his mother was well enough to come home, their apartment had been rented to another family. Jerry and his sister were never able to find out what had happened to their clothes, toys, and the only picture they had of their dad.

Jerry will always demand that people in his life behave pretty much the way *he* wants them to—for example, always be on time. He will do everything he can to be certain of it, including getting very angry when anyone else is late. He will even demand that other people keep the schedule he sets out for them. Some of his friends won't accept his need to be in control. He will reject those who won't go along.

Young people who have addicted parents hate the fact that they can never count on their parents. They desperately want to be able to count on things being the same day in and day out.

26. They experience a pervasive sense of guilt, shame, and embarrassment (Ellen Morehouse).

These kids believe that their parents drink or use drugs partly because they are such bad kids. That is especially true of kids who have two addicted parents. Psychologically, it works like this: "I can't blame Mom because I love her, I can't blame Dad because I love him, so it must be all my fault."

Case Study: Claire hated to hear her parents fight, hated the names they called each other, the things they said to each other. But they were at it again. When would it stop? Ever?

Finally she couldn't take it any more. "Please!" she begged, "can't you please stop? I'll do anything you want. I'll clean the house, I'll cook, I'll wash the dishes, I'll even wash the van. Just please stop!"

"Oh, shut up!" her father bellowed. "You're just like your mother! You're a good-for-nothing tramp! Who'd want to eat anything you cooked?"

It is embarrassing to live with an addict. Their friends, teachers, and everyone of their neighbors have been embarrassed. Sometimes the addict has embarrassed complete strangers. Children have difficulty separating themselves from their parents. In much the same way that a ten-year-old girl will be "embarrassed for" another ten-year-old who drops her tray in the school cafeteria, the child of an addict shares his parent's embarrassment. The addict's shame becomes his shame.

27. They tend to evaluate everything from an "all or none" perspective (Herbert Gravitz & Julie Bowden).

It is difficult for many of these children to understand that there is such a thing as moderation. They have lived with parents who think and act in extremes.

Case Study: Alice wanted a stepmother. Her mother had died when Alice was only two. The problem was that her father couldn't seem to find someone he could trust. He wanted someone who would do everything with the family. His ideal woman would be absolutely dedicated to family life.

When he met Jonne, he thought she was the one. She was beautiful, short, with green eyes and brown hair. She was very "family-oriented"—just what he wanted. After dating for several months, they moved to her house. Two weeks later, her father asked Jonne to marry him and she said, "Yes!"

Alice could hardly contain herself when she heard the news. Finally she would have a mother again. She had liked Jonne from the moment she met her. That day she told all her friends, teachers, even the cooks in the cafeteria.

But when she got home, something was wrong. She could tell it the minute she walked into the house. Her father was sitting there "all puffed up like a toad," which always meant he was angry. "What's wrong, Dad?" she asked.

"Honey," he said, "I'm not sure this is gonna work out with Jonne. Seems she's got a real independent streak in her. Not nearly as family-oriented as I thought."

"What happened?" asked Alice.

"Well, she wants to go back to school for a year or so. She'd be gone six hours a day. Two of them at night!"

"But it would only be for a year, Dad," she replied. "You could still marry her, couldn't you?"

"I've been looking for an apartment for us," he said. "I think we'd better wait until I feel more comfortable. My experience with women is that first it's school, then it's a movie, next it's a night out with the girls. Before you know it they're running around on you." He shook his head with the sure knowledge that he was right.

Alice knew that look. It was over. He'd be moving their stuff out tomorrow. He'd leave a note on the table. Probably pick her up after school to take her to their new apartment. Why did it always turn out this way? Why couldn't he pick someone who would stick with them? That night, she sat in her room with the lights out. She was too sad even to cry. It was the first time she thought about using drugs ...

These children grow into adulthood thinking that people are either good or bad, angry or happy, for them or against them. If they put a dent in their fender, the car is ruined; if they're late for work, they might as well stay home; if their spouse mentions that someone else is attractive, it means they are ugly.

28. They feel profoundly unlovable (Jane Middleton-Moz and Lorie Dwinell).

Children of addicts experience their parent's drug abuse as abandonment, and they blame themselves. Their reasoning goes like this: "I love my parents. So it can't be their fault that they're not here for me. Therefore, it must be my fault. Parents are supposed to love their children. Since they don't love me, it must be my fault. I am unlovable."

Case Study: Amy was one of the prettiest girls in the sixth grade. She was tall and blond and had blue eyes. She was also smart and had a great sense of humor. Despite this, she had gone with nine boys this year—and it wasn't even Christmas yet.

Her school counselor couldn't understand it. Each of these boys liked Amy well enough to ask her out, but every one had dropped her in less than a week. Why were they dumping her?

Then one day she overheard Amy talking to a girl-friend. "Why don't you go out with Derek?" said the girl. "He told me he likes you."

"Naw," said Amy. "That's just because he doesn't know me. If I went out with him, I'd just end up getting dumped. No one likes me who knows me."

"I like you," the girl said.

"That's just because you really don't know me," replied Amy. "Even my father doesn't love me. He hates me so much that he would rather stay out and drink half the night. He'd do anything to be away from me."

These kids carry around one of the worst self-images known to the human race. Don Ludlow, a counselor working at Hugs—an Oklahoma City program that works with children of alcoholics, says, "You can tell these kids believe they are 'lower than a centipede with fallen arches' by the way they act. I actually know one little girl who wrote Santa a note saying, 'You don't have to bring me anything this year. Give it to someone who's nice.'"

These young people will carry the scars of growing up with an addicted parent for the rest of their lives. It will affect their lives, their marriages, *and* their children. The pain and unhappiness will go on years beyond the time they leave their home and parents—unless they get treatment. That is discussed in Chapter 14.

CHAPTER 12

Can My Parent Get Well?

Recovery is a very complicated matter. On the most basic level, it involves reversing the psychological defenses employed to shield the addict against the emotional pain of his addiction. Those defenses are projection, blaming, displacement, rigidity, denial, minimization, repression of feelings, expression of anger, and blackouts with confabulation, the defenses described in Chapter 6.

In a very real sense, recovery is a journey, or a series of journeys, from those defensive ways of dealing with the world to a healthier way of being.

The Journey from Projection to Experiencing

The defense of projection is used to overcome the necessity of facing the emotional pain that addiction causes. In recovery, the addict quits projecting and actually begins to experience emotional pain the way a normal person would experience it.

Case Study: Brooke's father was an alcoholic. He had been through treatment and had been attending Alcoholics Anonymous for three years. He was an only child whose mother had died several years earlier. His father was quite old and becoming more and more senile daily.

One Saturday morning Brooke and her father were working outside, Dad mowing and Brooke edging the yard, when her mother came out and talked quietly to Dad. Brooke could see that Mom was upset, so she went to find out what was wrong.

Her mother was saying, "The police have your father. They found him wandering around, lost and disoriented, about a mile from his house. He couldn't tell them where he lived. We've got to do something to protect him from himself."

Brooke's father looked sad as he said, "I know. We have to put him in a nursing home. And I promised him I would never do that."

Brooke saw his hands tremble and knew that he was going to cry. "I hate so much to have to do that."

"I know, honey," Mom said, hugging her husband and beginning to cry, too. Brooke hugged them both, and they stood like that for a long time. Then they went to the police station together.

Sad as it was, the family in general and Brooke's dad in particular were acting in a *normal* way, responding to the situation normally, not as they would have if Dad had still been drinking.

The Journey from Rigidity to Growth

The defense of rigidity is used to deal with the inability of the addict to handle change. In recovery, the addict experiences change as a normal part of life. It is no longer feared as threatening. It may even be sought after.

Case Study: Brittany's father was addicted to speed. He had been in recovery for six years. He attended Narcotics Anonymous three times a week, working hard on his recovery. Mom attended Al-Anon, and Brittany went to regular meetings of Alateen.

Dad had been working for the Bentac Corporation for eight years and was senior account manager. He had lived in Fort Worth all his life.

One evening during dinner the phone rang. It was for Brittany's dad. "This is he," he said. "Yes, I've heard a lot of good things about your company . . . in Chicago . . . the vice presidency? . . . How much? . . . Are you *serious*? Yes, of course I'm interested . . . but give me some time . . . I need to think about this and talk to my family . . . I'll have an answer for you by Friday." He hung up the telephone, looking a little like a man who's been clipped by an iron pipe.

"That was Cletus Brown, president of Control Graphics in Chicago—I told you about meeting him last week. He has offered me the vice presidency of his company. It would be a $25,000 a year increase in salary. But it would mean moving to Chicago." He looked around the table at the astonished faces. "What do you think?"

"Oh, Tom," his wife said. "That would mean so many changes! At least, now I can talk about being afraid."

Brittany said, "I'd hate to leave all my friends and school and everything, but it might be fun living someplace else for a while, and I could always come back here to college. When you think of it, I've lived in this one house all my life."

"I'd like to give it a try," Tom said. "I might never get an opportunity like this again!"

Mom said, "I'll be supportive and go along. It just might be fun. It certainly will be different—and a change."

Her father laughed and said, "I can't believe I'm looking forward to this!"

Once, even with the salary increase, the job offer would have been a frightening threat.

The Journey from Denial to Honesty

Denial is a defense used to avoid knowing the extent of one's addiction. Denial also protects the addict from knowledge of the damage that is being done to self and others by the addiction.

Case Study: Amanda's mother is an alcoholic who joined Alcoholics Anonymous eighteen months ago. Since then life has become more and more normal—and happy—for all the family.

One morning Amanda opened the door to find her mother's friend, Mary, on the doorstep. Mary belonged to a social club that Amanda knew, from past experience, served booze by the gallon at their parties. Now Mary was asking Amanda's mom to help serve at a party coming up the next weekend.

Mom shook her head. "Look, Mary, I know those parties, and I know myself. I didn't even plan to go to the party."

"But Blanche, surely just once . . ."

"I know with that bunch it's hard to get a soft drink or something nonalcoholic, and I'm not going to take the risk just now. Later, when I feel on firmer ground, we'll see. But I'm afraid I'd start thinking that 'Just one drink won't hurt.' So, no, count me out."

When Mary had left—in a huff—Amanda raced to hug her mother. "I'm so proud of you, Mom. I was really afraid for a minute there . . ."

"Honey, so was I. That's why I said no. I've learned to be honest about and *with* myself and what I can and can't do."

The Journey from Blaming to Responsibility

The defense of blaming enables the addict to point a finger at someone else, thereby escaping responsibility for an irrational and damaging addiction. What the addict does not realize is that the very hand that points a finger at someone else has three fingers pointed backward right at the addict.

The author once received a notice from a car manufacturer saying, "A defect has been discovered in your model of car. Continued driving could result in injury or even death." The author was struck by the way fault was placed on the driver of the automobile, not the manufacturer who was ultimately responsible for the defect.

That is what the defense of blaming does. When an addict gets into recovery, he quits blaming and accepts responsibility for his own behavior.

Case Study: Brice's father is a recovering alcoholic. Life for all the family has been better and easier in the two years since he got treatment and joined Alcoholics Anonymous.

The family owns two rental houses. Over his mom's protests, Brice's dad had rented one of them to a cousin, even though the cousin had recently declared bankruptcy and had a long history of not working—not because he couldn't find a job but because he didn't look for one.

Five months later the cousin was three months behind on his rent and had been fired from two different jobs for absenteeism. He had also knocked a hole in a wall and broken two windows.

"What are we going to do now?" Brice's mom demanded. "That jerk is costing *us* a lot of money."

"I'm not sure," Dad said. "I'll tell him to move. I do know I made the decision, and I'll have to deal with the problem. It is my responsibility."

Brice remembers how at one time the responsibility for *any* problem in the family was enough to send his father into a binge.

The Journey from Displacement to Assertiveness

When an addict uses displacement as a psychological defense, he does so because he feels that he cannot confront the person with whom he is actually angry. That is because most addicts grew up with parents who were also addicts. In this sense they are very much like abused children who know only two roles: victim and victimizer.

They have experienced both of those roles. What they haven't experienced is that place in between, the healthy place called assertiveness. Assertiveness is not hostility. It is stating straightforwardly what one needs, wants, believes, and feels.

Case Study: Niki's mother went into treatment for alcoholism six months ago, and for Niki it has been like having a new person around the house. The most notable difference is that Niki is no longer the target of her mother's rages when things don't go well at work.

Mom works for a man who has a strong streak of sadistic bully in him. Nothing that goes wrong in the office is ever his fault. He takes out his temper on Niki's mom, who then used to spend the evening yelling at Niki, her father, and her big brother.

After treatment, the first time her boss threw a tantrum Niki's mom said, "Mr. Schneider, if you don't want mistakes in your letters, don't dictate them while you are trying to eat a doughnut. And don't yell at me again. You can treat me like an adult who is good at my job, or you can get another secretary."

The boss was so astonished that he spilled coffee down the front of his shirt, Mom was happy to note.

The next time he yelled at her, Niki's mother went to *his* boss, explained the situation, and said, "I like working for this company, and I want very much to stay. But if you can't find me another opening, I'm leaving. I refuse to be that man's emotional lightning rod any longer." The boss's boss moved her to another department.

Mom also apologized to Niki and the rest of the family. "I was doing the same thing to you that Schneider was doing to me—I just didn't realize it." Niki loved hearing the story. To her, Mom seemed like a heroine.

The Journey from Expression of Anger to Leveling

Addicts most often employ the psychological defense of expression of anger in order not to deal with the pain of a life that is out of control.

The persons closest to an addict are the very ones most often victimized by the addict's anger. Such a small thing as a daughter's saying, "Do you want to see my class picture?" can trigger an explosion: "Do you think that's all I've got to do with my time? You sit around all day in school flirting with boys while I work my behind off to support you and that lazy good-for-nothing mother of yours. You're no good, just like her! Why don't you do something useful for a change, like cook dinner or do the laundry?"

Of course, *not* showing Dad the school picture could just as easily have drawn, "Didn't bother to show me your school picture, huh? What's the matter, I'm not important enough? Is that it? You'll show other people, but don't bother with the person who works his butt off so you can pay for things like that . . ." The child of an addict can't win, no matter what he or she may do.

What the addict is feeling is stress. If he were to level with his daughter, or the world in general, there would be a real chance of getting the help he needs.

Case Study: Celeste's father was a heroin addict. He had had only two months of being straight, but he was really working the Narcotics Anonymous program. His sponsor had recommended that he attend ninety meetings in ninety days. He was also working as much overtime as possible to pay his hospital bill for treatment. He had almost no time to himself. In the past any request for time would have triggered an irrational outburst of anger.

Celeste wanted to ask him to come to the Homecoming football game. She was also very much afraid to ask. Still, he was behaving so differently since treatment that she decided to take the risk. "Dad, would you come to the game this Saturday? It's Homecoming, and I am first runner-up to the homecoming queen."

"I know, and I'm very proud of you," Dad said. "I'd

like very much to go, but I just can't. The only meeting I can attend is during the game. I'm too new at being off that garbage to risk falling back now. I'll miss being there, and I'll be thinking about you."

Celeste did miss her dad at the game, but somehow she felt right about his not being there. He had leveled with her, and he was working hard to stay straight.

The Journey from Minimization to Acceptance

The defense of minimization is usually employed by the addict in an effort to avoid painful realization of life. In recovery, the addict begins to accept himself as a human being who sometimes makes mistakes. Mistakes are accepted as part of life. Making mistakes doesn't mean he is bad, only human. Acceptance means that he is less judgmental of others.

Case Study: Teresa's mom had been addicted to a variety of drugs. She had gone through treatment and aftercare and was currently active in Narcotics Anonymous. A single parent, she had been straight for almost two years.

On vacation Teresa and her mom went to the mountains about five hundred miles from home. Teresa was in charge of reading the map, and her mother drove.

Everything seemed to go wrong. The road got worse and worse, narrow and full of holes. Then it just ended, running out in a patch of pine trees in sandy-looking ground.

Teresa's mom said, "Do you have any idea where we are?"

"Well—I'd say lost. I'm sorry, Mom. I *thought* I knew where we were."

"Well, we'll just have to go back to someplace we recognize and try again." But as Mom tried to turn the car the rear wheels slipped off into the deep sand and got stuck.

After a few minutes of trying to get the car out and realizing they couldn't, Mom said, "I guess we'll just have to walk out and get help."

Teresa began to cry. "Oh, Mom, I'm so sorry. It's all my fault." Once Mom would have agreed with that, and probably at the top of her lungs. Now she laughed and tousled Teresa's hair. "Don't be silly, honey. You got us lost, and I got us stuck. I'll rest a lot easier when we reach civilization and get someone to pull us out of this mess, but the walking out will be an adventure. After all, what's a camping trip for but adventure?"

The Journey from Confabulation to Admission

Confabulation is the defense employed to deal with the fear of insanity caused by blackouts from excessive drug or alcohol use.

Episodes of amnesia are extremely frightening. Most addicts fear that they are losing their mind. Everyone knows exactly where the addict was and what he or she did and said—except the addict. It is especially scary when the addict was sober.

Addicts react to that fear by "filling in the blanks" or inventing a story of where they were, what they did, and what they said. That is confabulation.

In recovery, the addict admits that he or she has no memory of things that occurred during the blackouts. The good news is that in recovery blackouts happen less and less frequently until for most addicts they subside altogether.

Case Study: Rose's dad was addicted to cocaine, marijuana, and alcohol. He had been through treatment twice. This time it seemed to be working. He had been sober and straight and attending Narcotics Anonymous for three months. He still experienced blackouts, but they were farther apart and shorter than in the beginning.

One morning he told Rose not to take the bus after school because he would pick her up and take her to visit her grandmother that evening. When school let out, Rose waited for her father—who did not show up. After half an hour she went to the principal's office and called him. "Why didn't you come and get me?" she asked.

He sounded blank on the other end of the line. "Why didn't you take the bus?"

"You told me that you were going to pick me up and we were going to Grandmother's."

"I said that? Oh—baby, I'm so sorry! I guess I've had another blackout. I'll come and get you right away. I wonder if I told your grandmother, or *what* I told her. I'll call her as soon as I pick you up."

The Journey from Repression of Feelings to Intimacy

Addicts repress all feelings except anger because getting in touch even with positive feelings also gets them in touch with the pain of addiction. In recovery, they learn once again to express the full range of emotions. That leads to the development of intimate relationships.

Case Study: Martin's mother was addicted to Xanax, a prescription drug. She had been in recovery for two and a half months.

She hadn't cried since she was a teenager. She wasn't even sure if she still could cry. In fact, she didn't feel much of anything—not sadness, not happiness, not even love. She wondered if she ever would feel anything again.

She had started using Valium when she was thirteen and switched to Xanax when she was thirty. The years between seemed to her a sort of sleepwalk. She had gone through them like a robot, seeing everything but feeling nothing. As a result, there was an enormous emotional distance between herself and her husband and children.

Martin and his mother were washing his dad's car, as a surprise for him. Their dog Hershey (Martin had named him Hershey because he was always giving kisses) was playing in the water and around their feet. When they started to dry the car, Hershey grabbed the towel and ran toward the street, with Martin in hot pursuit.

But Hershey ran right into the path of a car coming around the corner and was hit. Martin and his mother both screamed and ran to scoop him up. "Please, take us to the veterinarian's office!" Mom asked the driver of the car, which had stopped.

"Of course. Get in."

In the car Martin's mom was astonished to realize that she was holding Hershey and petting him—and crying.

It seemed like an eternity while they waited at the vet's office. Then the doctor came out with a big grin on her face. "He's going to be stiff and sore for a while, but no major damage was done. He'll be just fine."

They all hugged each other and laughed and cried—Martin, his mom, the vet, and the stranger who had been driving the car.

Only later did Martin's mother realize how odd it was that she had had to learn, all over again, to feel the emotions felt by the stranger—who had never seen any of them *or* Hershey before.

When they got home they laughed when they saw that

Martin's dad had awakened from his Saturday afternoon nap and was standing in the driveway staring at his water-spotted car and the water running down the street because no one had thought to shut it off.

Martin's mother hugged him and said, "I know this may sound silly, but I've never felt more in love with you than I do at this minute."

At first Dad looked confused; then he smiled and hugged her back and said, "I've waited a long time to hear you say that. You don't know how good it sounds."

His parents went into the house, and Martin began to rewash the car—dancing and singing as he worked.

CHAPTER 13

Living with What You Can't Change

Sometimes, no matter how hard you try to make a difference, one or both of your parents will continue to practice his or her addiction.

When that happens the question quickly becomes, "How can I live with this?" It is an extremely important question. The majority of addicts do continue to practice their addiction until it kills them. So learning to live with it may be your only alternative.

Learning to live with addicted parents may be the most difficult challenge any child or adolescent ever has to face. It is important for you to understand that your actions will have a tremendous impact on your ability to survive the experience in the most positive way possible. Here are some do's and don'ts.

DO'S

1. Find friends who are healthy. One or two good friends can make a big difference in your being able to release

some of the stress under which you live. You will be able to share feelings openly, and that is productive for your growth as a person.

Remember, in addicted families emotions and feelings are usually repressed. It is extremely important for you to develop outlets with whom you can express your feelings.

Other characteristics of healthy friendships are honesty, loyalty, equality, consideration, openness, acceptance, and kindness.

2. Start a journal or diary. Developing the habit of writing regularly in a journal can be extremely helpful.

There are several methods of keeping a journal. One method is simply to note the important events of each day. A more helpful method is to address each entry to a particular person—a friend, a relative, or the person who plays the greatest role in that entry. Recount the events of the day or incident, then be sure to express how you felt during those events.

Be sure to keep your diary or journal in a safe place! Alcoholic or addicted family members often have little sense of personal boundaries. Someone in your family might read it, and that could be embarrassing or subject you to abuse.

3. Visit your school counselor. Most school counselors are professionals who are trained to help students deal with the difficulties of life in general and living with addicted parents in particular. They can help you get a new perspective on your problems.

Be willing to attend enough sessions so that you and the counselor can get to know each other. It can be frightening to think about baring your soul to someone you hardly know, but participating in counseling can be an extremely enriching experiencing.

4. Attend Alateen. Few experiences are more healing than participating in Alateen meetings. There you will find other teens who come from addicted families. It is very healing to share your worst fear—believing yourself to be the only person who has that fear—only to have two other teenagers say, "I've worried about the same thing."

Alateen is called a Twelve-Step Recovery Program because the focus is on helping people work though to a place of health. If you attend meetings regularly and sincerely work the program, your rewards will be great.

One of the great things about Alateen is that you will develop a group of friends you can call in a crisis. That can be a significant step in ending your isolation, perhaps forever.

5. Make a list of all your good points. (If you need to, get a friend to help you.) Most children growing up in addicted families have very low self-esteem. It may be hard for them to realize that they do have good points. That's why making a list can be so enlightening.

In the author's experience, teens growing up in addicted family systems have some strengths that other teens don't have. For example, they are usually able to cope with crises, they are survivors, and they can be highly self-sufficient. Making a list of your good points will help you to maintain a healthy balance within yourself.

6. Call a Certified Drug and Alcohol Counselor. If you can find one who is willing to spend some time talking to you on the phone about your problems, you may be able

to get answers to many of the things that mystify you about your family.

Most of these counselors have either lived with an addicted person or been addicted themselves. They know the problems from personal experience. Most of them will be happy to talk to you.

7. Arrange for an intervention. When you talk to the Certified Drug and Alcohol Counselor, ask about the possiblity of arranging an intervention for your addicted parent. Before you do that, read Chapter 14 of this book and make a list of questions you would like the counselor to answer.

An intervention is designed to get your addicted parent into treatment as soon as possible. It could work for your parent, and the counselor will probably be glad to help you with it. If not, he will refer you to someone who can.

8. Attend a summer camp. It can be helpful to have a break from living with an addicted parent. Most summer camps have trained counselors on staff. Be sure to seek them out and talk to them about the problems in your family.

Although the cost of summer camp can be prohibitive, scholarships are often available. Ask the organization that is advertising the camp you wish to attend about scholarship opportunities.

9. Participate in church or synagogue. Regular participation in religious organizations can be helpful. Most pastors, priests, and rabbis entered the clergy because they wanted to be helpful to others. They would welcome the opportunity to talk with you. In addition, most religious

organizations have youth programs and youth leaders who take an interest in teenagers.

Although there are no guarantees, you may develop friendships with people your age who have a whole new perspective on your problems, and you may be able to help them with some of theirs. Remember, you do have strengths that others don't have.

Perhaps most important, you will have an opportunity to develop a strong faith relationship with God. Many adolescents growing up in addicted family systems have felt abandoned by everyone but God. Developing this relationship can make a great difference in how you deal with stress.

10. Find a hobby you enjoy. Collecting stamps, coins, marbles, dolls, insects, or baseball cards can help you focus your mind, energy, and emotions on something other than family problems.

Activities such as sewing, making home movies, taking pictures, operating a Citizens Band radio, star-gazing, or building model airplanes can be a great diversion. A bonus of pursuing a hobby can be finding new friends with similar interests.

11. Participate in sports. Games such as basketball, football, baseball, soccer, tennis, and volleyball can be a great way to get involved with people your age. Team sports help to develop discipline, cooperation, and identification.

Nonteam sports such as bicycling, swimming, diving, hiking, jogging, and weight lifting can also take your mind off your problems and increase your physical well-being. Activities such as band, pep club, and chorus may also serve this purpose.

12. Join a youth organization. The numerous youth organizations include Scouts, Campfire, Big Brothers, Big Sisters, 4-H, FFA, and church youth groups.

The benefits of participating in a youth organization include focusing your energy outside the home, gaining a commitment and sense of belonging to something outside of yourself, and helping you to maintain objectivity about your life.

13. Visit with relatives. One of the great things about our society before the Industrial Revolution was that most of the members of the extended family (aunts, uncles, cousins, and grandparents) lived close to each other. That made visiting easy. Teenagers were able to benefit from relationships with older cousins, aunts, uncles, and especially grandparents.

One way for this to happen today is for teenagers to make extended visits to favorite relatives. It can also help in keeping a perspective on your problems at home.

DON'TS

1. Don't make excuses for your addicted parents. That only protects them from the consequences of their behavior. Every time you excuse a parent for being drunk by saying, "Oh, he's been under a lot of stress at work lately," you provide another reason to get drunk the next time he is under stress. Every time you lie to a parent's employer by saying, "Dad's sick and can't come to work today," you ensure that the employer will have a harder time confronting your father for being too drunk to work.

These actions are called enabling behaviors because they allow an addicted person to continue practicing his addiction. It is far better to stop all enabling behaviors, thereby allowing the addict to suffer the consequences of his behavior.

2. Don't try to "fix" your parent. Trying to fix an addicted parent doesn't work for many reasons. The first is because it isn't your job. It is a parent's job to fix himself.

The second reason is that it is based on faulty logic. It is not your fault that your parent is addicted. If you try to fix your parent, you well may end up accepting major responsibility for his condition or actions. Remember, your parent is addicted because he has inherited a genetic tendency to addiction.

The third reason that you shouldn't try to fix your parent is that teenagers tend to become overinvolved in their parents' lives, thus losing a large part of their own lives. Children need to be children, and teenagers need to be teenagers. You experience this time of your life only once!

3. Don't attack or criticize an addicted parent. Remember that addicts have a very rigid defense system. When criticized, they first respond by feeling guilty. Then almost immediately they become defensive and begin to rationalize and justify their addictive behavior. Criticism merely deepens their defense mechanisms and eventually leads to a higher level of addiction.

It is best to talk to an addict about what you feel. Start by saying, "I feel sad, alone, left out." In that way the addict may be able to hear what your pain is about and not take it personally.

4. Don't blame the addicted parent. Blame the mood-altering drug or behavior. The addicted parent did not choose to be addicted; he was predisposed to become

addicted. When he is less filled with guilt, he may be able to be more objective. That could be the first step toward his seeking help for his addiction.

5. Don't set up your own abuse. Many addicts are violent. Those who are not are often verbally abusive. If you know that a certain behavior will set your parent into a sequence of abuse, avoid that behavior.

If you take time to think, you may be able to forestall much of your own emotional or physical pain. It may not be easy to identify which of your actions or words sets up the abuse. For instance, some addicts become abusive when a son or daughter seems to cower, whereas others react when a son or daughter stands up to them. Once you figure out what sets the abusive cycle in motion, you will have much more power to prevent it.

6. Don't wallow in self-pity. Although you may have plenty of reason to feel sorry for yourself, it seldom accomplishes anything more than further lowering your self-image. It is better to focus on positive possibilities. Giving energy to the negative forces in your life gives *them* power. If you focus on the positive things in your life, you give them power. Like energy attracts like energy. Concentrate on the positive side of life. Don't fuel the negative aspects any more than necessary.

7. Don't experiment with mood-altering drugs or behaviors. Remember, if one of your parents has a genetic predisposition toward addiction, you probably have it too. Some teenagers are absolutely defenseless against addiction. As there are do's and don't in dealing with the addiction of your parents, there are also things you need

to do to avoid your own addiction and, eventually, the addiction of your children.

By now it should be clear to the reader that most addiction is inherited, not developed. It is also clear that children of addicts have a host of emotional difficulties developed by growing up with an addicted parent. These emotional problems are passed on from generation to generation.

Given these facts, the thoughtful reader may be wondering about several issues: How can I avoid being addicted? Can I drink socially? Will I marry an addict? Will my children be doomed to repeat my parents' addiction problems? What about their children? Are any of us truly safe?

If one of your parents is an addict, you have a 50 percent chance of becoming an addict. If both of your parents are addicts, your odds could be as high as 75 percent. If your father was addicted at a very young age, was violent when drinking, and you are a male, your odds are as high as 90 percent. In fact, some people are absolutely defenseless against addiction from the moment they first use a mood-altering chemical. For many of you, your only defense against addiction is never to use or drink.

That makes it very important to discover whether anybody in your family is or was addicted. Since you are reading a book about drug-addicted parents, the answer may be obvious. But even if you are reading merely for information, you could end up addicted if a grandparent or great grandparent was addicted. And that's something that may not be known.

It operates like heredity in breeding animals. If a white dog and a black dog mate, you usually get one white puppy, one black puppy, and two black-and-white puppies. If one of the black puppies grows up and mates with a black dog, they may have three black puppies and one black-and-white puppy.

Even if all of the black puppies grow up to mate with black dogs, it is possible for a black-and-while puppy to be born several generations later. If we let the whiteness represent the gene that passes on addiction, you can see that it is likely that some people will be prone to addiction for several generations. Therefore, if you have had an addict in the family you should never drink or use a mood-altering chemical, because you might be the person who is carrying that gene. Unlike the puppies in our example, you can't tell that just by looking!

Even if you never use a mood-altering chemical, there is still a good possibility that you will pass on the genetic potential toward addiction to your children, and they will pass it on to theirs. You should help make sobriety a way of life in your family.

When you have children, you should start to educate them very early. It is known that 33 percent of all fourth-graders feel under pressure to use a mood-altering chemical, and 50 percent of all sixth-graders feel so pressured. So develop a drug-free lifestyle that involves healthy ways of feeling good about yourself.

This is crucial for you and all of your potential offspring —now and forever. The whole world, including you and me and our families, would be better off if we avoided all forms of mood-altering drugs.

CHAPTER 14

What to Do When You Can't Live with It

Many people your age who are living with a drug-abusing parent feel trapped, unable to do anything. This chapter is about the things that can bring you to the point of losing your mind or thinking of suicide or homicide—and what you can do instead.

Growing up in an addicted family is an endless nightmare. If you've lived in one, no one needs to tell you that. But there is a point at which it descends from nightmare into hell itself; and when you reach that point, you must do something to save your sanity—perhaps your life.

Child Abuse

There are several kinds of child abuse, some worse than others. The degree depends on: (1) how severe the abuse is; (2) how well you handle the abuse; (3) your age when it started; (4) how long it goes on; and (5) how other adults, including your other parent, deal with it when they find out.

Case Study: Josey was seventeen when her father left her mother and moved into an apartment. Before that, there had been numerous fights over her mother's drinking, but Josey had been able to avoid being involved in most of them.

After the separation, her father asked her to live with him. It was tempting, but Josie liked her school, and someone needed to take care of her mother. So she stayed where she was. "In another year and a half, I'll be going to college," she said to her father.

"All right," he said. "I just want you to know you are wanted. If anything changes, or if your mother gets so bad that you can't take it, all you need to do is call." They left it at that.

But with her father gone, her mother's drinking rapidly got worse. She was drunk every afternoon when Josey came home. The smell of whiskey was everywhere in the house. And Josey was becoming more and more concerned about her mother's health.

Finally, Josey could stand it no longer. "Mother," she said, "you've got to get a grip on yourself. You're drinking away your health and your future. You've got to slow . . . "

"Slow, what?" shouted her mother. "Why, you ungrateful little snip! I put up with all that baloney from your father. Who do you think I did that for, myself? I did it for you! I would have left him fifteen years ago if it wasn't for you!"

"Mother," Josey said angrily, "you're losing touch with reality. It was Dad who left you, remember?"

"Damn you! "I'll teach you to run that smart little

mouth of yours!" She knocked Josey to the floor and was on top of her instantly, scratching and pulling her hair.

Josey finally managed to free herself and ran from the house in her bare feet, clothes half torn off. She ran about two blocks to the pay phone at the convenience store, where she called her father. When he answered, she told him what had happened.

"Are you okay?" he asked.

"Yes," she replied. "Just a few scratches and some missing hair. But I'm scared, Dad. She's getting worse by the day!"

"Where are you?" he asked.

"I'm at that little store, you know, the 'Get & Go'," she said.

"Stay where you are," he said; "I'll be right there."

It seemed as if she had just hung up when the squeal of tires announced her father's arrival. The door was open and he was running toward her. "It's all right now," he said. "You're coming with me. Everything will be okay."

"But what will become of Mom? She's killing herself, Dad!"

"I'm going to take care of that right now," he said. "If I hadn't been such a coward, I'd have straightened this out years ago." He picked up the receiver of the pay phone, punched in a number and waited. "Sam, you got a bed ready? Good. See you in about thirty minutes!" Then he clicked the receiver down briefly and dialed again. "John," he said, "can you meet me at my place right away? Great!" Turning to Josey, he said, "Let's go."

"Where are we going?" she asked.

With more determination in his voice than she had ever heard, he said, "Home, where we belong."

When they got back to the house, her mother was

standing in the kitchen pouring a drink. She raised the glass to her lips as she turned toward them.

"Enjoy that one," Josey's father said. "It will be the last one you ever have!"

Startled, she dropped the glass and staggered backward. "Just what do you think . . . "

Josey's scream interrupted her, "Daddy, no!"

He looked at Josey, "Oh, I'm not going to hit her—not that I wouldn't like to!"

Then, looking directly into his wife's eyes, he said, "You've got two choices. By this time John Welch and his squad car are waiting outside. You're going to get into that car. He will take you either to jail where you will be charged with child abuse, or to Valley Green where you will receive treatment for alcoholism. You can get in the car like a lady, or John will put you in like a criminal."

She walked out of the house, paused to look back at Josey, and got into the car.

John shut her door, got in, and said, "Where will it be, Mrs. Kelso?"

"Treatment," she said.

In this case, the victim was almost eighteen. She was able to deal with the abuse by calling her father. He handled the situation well: He took charge, put an end to the abuse, and got the offender into treatment.

Not all victims are so fortunate. Sometimes a single act of abuse is so violent that the victim is severely damaged. Sometimes the abuse goes on, spiraling into more and more destructive levels. Sometimes the nonabusing parent is too damaged from drugs or her own abuse to intervene. When that is the case, the victim can be horribly damaged.

Case Study: Beretta was four years old when her step-father began abusing her. He was a methamphetamine user who sometimes got very angry and violent—often hitting and kicking her. She had been bruised, cut, and had suffered broken bones. But each time her mother took her to the hospital or to a doctor, she lied about how she had been hurt.

One afternoon when she was seven, he came home early to find her sitting at the kitchen table doing homework. As he stood over her, he seemed agitated and angry. "What ya doing, sweet thing?" he asked loudly.

Beretta knew he was high, and this frightened her; he only hurt her when he was doing drugs. "My lessons," she replied.

He went into the living room without saying a word.

She could hear him putting a videotape into the VCR. She hated those movies he sometimes made her watch—always people with their clothes off. Thinking that she had better leave, she said, "I'm finished. I think I'll go over to Tommy's house for a while."

"What's Tommy got that I ain't got?" he asked.

"Nothing," she said. "But I promised to help him with his homework."

"Yeah, right!" he said. "Well, before you go, come here and help me with *my* homework."

Slowly, Beretta walked into the living room. When she saw that he was undressed, she turned to leave.

"And don't turn your back on me, you little creep," he shouted. "I said, 'Come here.'"

"I'm afraid," she said.

"This is nothing to be afraid of," he said. "It will be fun." He grabbed her, pulled her onto his lap, and ripped her clothes off. Then he raped her.

It was the worst pain she had ever felt. "Stop!" she screamed. "You are hurting me."

"Shut your mouth, or I'll kill you!" he said. When it was over, he dragged her to the bathtub, filled it with water, and threw her into it. "You need a bath," he said. "You're dirty. Don't get out of there until I tell you to get out." Then he left the room.

She was still in the tub two hours later when her mother got home. "What's going on here?" she said.

Beretta sobbed out the whole story.

Her mother's reaction? "This would never have happened if you hadn't started it! You got exactly what you had coming!"

From that point on, her stepfather raped her at least once a week until she was sixteen. That year, he made her pregnant.

After the baby was born, Beretta shared a hospital room with another unwed mother, Virginia. They hit it off right away, and Beretta felt she could trust her new friend. So she told her everything. And Virginia told a nurse. The nurse called the police.

Her stepfather and her mother are now in prison. He was sentenced to 100 years with no possibility of parole. He will die in prison. Her mother is serving ten years. She will be eligible for parole in three. Beretta will need many years of counseling before she can expect to lead even a half-way normal existence.

Note: Methamphetamine often causes the user to be extremely violent and sometimes sexually aggressive. This has become epidemic. For example, in 1992 in San Diego, 24 percent of all people arrested for violent crimes were under the influence of this drug when they committed the crime. If someone is abusing you who is also using speed, run—don't walk—to the nearest police officer. Many thousands of children—some only a few months old—have been raped, permanently injured, or beaten to death by someone on speed.

Neglect is failure to provide food, clothing, shelter, or protection for a child by the persons responsible for that child's care.

Case Study: Miska is ten years old. She has never been lucky enough to be sure that she would be fed. Her mother is addicted to heroin, and she always buys her drugs first. Whatever is left goes for the family's needs.

Miska doesn't remember her father. When she was two years old, he died in a fire along with her only sister. Her mother was stoned when it happened. She had been trying to cook breakfast, but had gotten sleepy and sat down to rest. She "nodded off," only to awake to find the house in flames. She was the only one who got out. Miska was born that very afternoon.

Since that time, her mother has been even more obsessed with heroin. Sometimes Miska thinks her mother uses it to avoid feeling the guilt of causing the fire.

Verbal abuse is the action of a parent or someone in authority being overcritical or threatening a child in such a way that the child is emotionally damaged.

Case Study: Damont is the victim of his "father's" verbal abuse. His parents were engaged to be married when a man broke into his mother's room one night and raped her, making her pregnant. His father was deeply in love with his mother and married her just the same, but when he drinks—and he does that more and more—he calls Damont names.

His father should have sought counseling. He has not been able to accept Damont as his son. But mostly he is angry that the police never caught the rapist. So he takes out the anger on the rapist's son—which is also Damont.

Damont feels that he did something terribly wrong, but he doesn't know what to do about it.

Physical abuse is when a parent, adult, or someone in authority hits, kicks, burns, twists, or shakes you in such a way that your body is, or could have been, damaged.

Case Study: Juno is fifteen. He is tall, dark, and, according to the girls in his class, "a real babe." They love the way his eyes flash when he talks. They would be surprised to discover that he is being abused by his alcoholic uncle, Juan. Last week, Juan tied him to a chair and burned him on the chest with a red-hot poker from the fireplace. Then he put out his cigarette on Juno's arm.

Sexual abuse is when an adult, parent, or someone in authority engages in sexual behavior with a minor. Even if the minor has given consent, it is not acceptable as a defense by an adult. It also makes no difference whether the abuse is in the form of fondling the victim's private parts, having intercourse, or suggesting those behaviors.

Case Study: Marti is thirteen. Her brother, Frank, who is seventeen, has been sexually abusing her since she was ten. Every night after their parents are asleep, he goes into her room and has sex with her. Frank has told her that he will cut off her cat's head if she tells.

Marti doesn't know that Frank is an addict and a dealer.

He uses and sells crack cocaine. Their older brother, Jason, died from using crack.

Addiction often fuels these kinds of abuse. Children who have been abused are afraid to tell for a number of reasons. The simplest is knowing that when their abuser gets out of jail the abuse may get worse. The most complex is that they often still love their mom, dad, brother, or whoever the abuser is.

Family loyalty—and remember that children of addicts can be extremely loyal—also comes into play. It is not always loyalty to the abusing parent. Sometimes kids don't want to tell on a parent because they don't want to hurt the nonabusing parent.

Case Study: Jennifer had been molested by her pot-smoking father for over a year before she finally broke down and told a teacher about it. "I can't turn him in," she wailed tearfully. "He'd go to jail, and then what would happen to us? We barely get by as it is, and Mom's so helpless I don't think she's capable of going to the store for a loaf of bread by herself. You've got to promise you won't tell anyone!"

Unfortunately, Jennifer was right. Families can and do wind up on welfare and homeless when parents go to jail for such crimes. Abusers often use that fear to control victims, to keep them from reporting the abuse. "If you tell, they'll separate all you kids, farm you out to foster homes; you'll never see each other again. Your mom will wind up on the streets. We'll lose the house."

And that does happen! Social services people and the law itself have been known to be both heartless and brainless in the handling of such families, seeming to care more about guarding themselves against possible criticism than doing what is best for the emotional welfare of the children involved.

Blowing the Whistle Without Blowing Your Life!

In many ways, when you decide to tell is an individual matter. Remember, the issue is not *whether* you should tell someone, but when and whom you should tell.

You must tell someone for your own sake as well as that of your brothers and sisters. Few walk away from such a situation without emotional scars.

The big question is: How can you do it with the least risk of everyone's life being torn apart? Sometimes you can't, but sometimes you can do something to make things better.

Alternatives

One thing that could help is talking to your minister, priest, or rabbi. This could be a smart or a dumb idea, depending on the clergyperson. Some have training in dealing with emotional problems, and some don't. Some, in fact, might come totally unglued at hearing that your father or mother is a child abuser. It probably comes down to using your own best judgment.

When they are trained, they can be very helpful. Your clergyperson can help you deal with your parents, the problems from the abuse, and even find a safe place for you to stay if you need one.

A second plan, depending on how much leverage you have, is to get the abuser to go for treatment. Most professionals who treat these cases know that this leverage can be considerable. Many people who love their children end up abusing them. Often it is not lack of love that causes the abuse, but lack of coping and parenting skills. In these cases, the family may be able to talk the abuser into seeking help. It almost always goes better for the abuser in particular, and the family in general, if a counselor can call Child Protective Services to say that an abuser has voluntarily come for help. If the abuse has not been severe, the agency often allows the case to ride with a competent professional. If therapy is successful, the abuser may not be charged or may receive a deferred sentence. It is possible that the family will remain intact, in which case everybody wins: The abuse stops, the child is protected, the parents get a better marriage, no one goes to jail, and no one is placed in foster care. The court or Child Protective Services will probably monitor the family for a time, but that can be helpful when handled well.

In more severe cases in which the family must be broken up by the imprisonment of the abuser, the court may take control of all children under the age of eighteen. They will be placed in a "children's home" or foster care. If that is a concern for you, here are a few ideas that might work.

Get a relative to take over the family care for a while—an aunt, perhaps, or grandparents. Sometimes even an older brother or sister is considered mature enough to be a guardian. If you have a relative or friend that you trust, talk to him or her before you talk to the law. Having someone go with you to the police station to assure them that the family is being cared for may prevent your being forced into some kind of "protective" situation. They will almost always defer to a relative.

Contact your religious organization. Many have resources with which to help families—shelters, financial aid, and so on. If one of these agencies is taking care of your family, it is possible that the law will not step in and make you wards of the court.

Make the point that your nonabusing parent could care for the children. Children are taken away from home in such situations because the police assume—sometimes correctly—that the nonabusing parent knew about it and made no effort to stop it. This is not always the case, however. And even when it is, oversight by the court may help make this work.

All of this certainly is not meant to make the legal process and the police sound like the enemy. In this case the enemy is at home, not here. But everyone has heard horror stories, a lot of them are true, and the resulting fear keeps many kids from telling what is happening to them. That is something that social services people should understand: Bad as things are at home, they are at least a known factor. What will happen after the kid blows the whistle is not known. The devil that you don't know is always more frightening than the devil that you do know.

Getting Treatment

Sometimes, the only real problem is the addiction of one of your parents. If you've read the rest of this book, you know that can be a big enough problem in itself. When it is the issue, get help.

The best way to begin is to call a chemical dependency treatment center or a certified alcohol and drug counselor. Say that you have a parent who is addicted. The counselor will probably ask some questions, mainly why you think your parent is an addict. Once he or she is satisfied that you are right, an appointment will probably be made for you to come in to talk with the counselor.

It is possible that an intervention will be arranged.

The Intervention

Intervention is a technique designed to break through the addict's denial and get him or her to accept help. It takes coordination and effort to arrange an effective intervention. First you need to give the counselor the names and telephone numbers of other people who are interested in getting your addicted parent to quit. The counselor calls the people on the list and asks them to the next appointment. He or she will probably find out what kind of drug or alcohol treatment policy your parent's employer has. Many companies give employees time off for addiction treatment. Often, the parent's boss wants to be part of the intervention.

If there is no such policy, the counselor asks questions to discover whether the employer will be helpful and may invite him to participate in the intervention.

Next the counselor trains those who are to take part in the intervention. It is important that the confrontation be loving, a genuine attempt to help. A hostile confrontation would only raise the addict's defenses, making help less likely.

On the day of the intervention, the participants meet at the counselor's office or at the addict's home. The deciding factor is often whether the addict is an early morning user. If so, it is better to have the intervention at home before use can occur. Intervention works best when the addict is not stoned. Almost certainly the addict is surprised and, at first, not at all pleased.

The counselor starts by saying something like, "Bill, we are all here today because we care about what's happening to you. We would like you to sit down and listen. You can talk after we've each had a turn."

Each person in turn says something like, "Bill, I love you, but this is what I've noticed." He or she then states one or two actions that the addict did while was under the influence of alcohol or drugs. It is important to blame the alcohol or drug, not the addict.

Then the counselor says, "Now each of us will tell you what we think needs to happen for you, and what we need for ourselves if you don't accept our advice."

At this point, each person says "Bill, will you please go to treatment? If you don't, what I need is to ——." It is important that each person state a real need, one that he or she will actually fulfill if Bill does not go to treatment. The boss may say, "You've been a good employee, but if you don't go to treatment, I will have to fire you." His wife may say, "Bill, I love you, but I can't go on like this. If you don't get treatment, I am going to divorce you." A child may say, "I love you, Dad, but I've been frightened too many times by your driving. If you don't go to treatment, I can't ride with you anymore." A sister may say, "Bill, I love you. You're my only brother. But if you don't go to treatment, you're not welcome in my home any more."

Usually, with his or her support system folding up under him, the addict accepts treatment. At this point, the addict is taken immediately to a treatment center.

The Treatment Center

Chemical dependency treatment centers are hospitals for addicts. They may be a part of a larger hospital, or separate units.

Usually treatment takes about a month. It consists of

lectures, counseling (group, individual, and family), required assignments, and attendance at self-help group meetings (discussed later in this chapter).

Family Week

An important part of the treatment program is family week, usually held during the third week, when the entire family is asked to participate. Some studies show that the success rate climbs from 33 percent to 90 percent when the family participates. So crucial is this that some treatment centers make it a condition of treatment.

After family week the addict, his counselor, and other treatment staff arrive at a discharge plan. The plan may have many elements, including a change of employment or living situations. It may include continued family therapy.

It will certainly include aftercare and family attendance at self-help groups.

Aftercare

Most treatment centers require attendance at aftercare for the addict and perhaps for the family. Aftercare, a therapy group run by a drug and alcohol counselor, usually meets once a week. Its purpose is to continue working through issues that were not completed during hospitalization and to help the addict and his family adjust to new ways of being together.

One of the important components of both aftercare and self-help groups is continuing support for the addict while his brain chemistry returns to normal, or as close to normal as possible, depending on the type of drug and length of time used. It takes at least two years and as long as five years for the brain to produce enough normal chemicals for the addict to feel good naturally. Support during this period is crucial. Most addicts who relapse do so in the first two years.

Self-Help Groups

These groups are often called twelve-step groups because they employ twelve steps to help members *continue their journey into health*. They are:

Alcoholics Anonymous (AA) for alcoholics.
Narcotics Anonymous (NA) for drug addicts.
Cocaine Anonymous (CA) for cocaine users.
Al-Anon for the addict's spouse.
Alateen for the addict's teenagers.
Alatot for the addict's children.
Adult Children of Alcoholics (ACA) for the adult children of alcoholics.
Children of Alcoholics (CA) for the children of addicts.

A few other self-help groups have emerged during the last few years. One of the more important is Rational Recovery, which is designed for those who do not like the spirituality of the above groups.

Another strong development is that of the Christian Twelve–Step Movement, which was developed by people who felt that the above groups were not Christian enough. Many churches now have these groups as a part of their regular ministry.

If you live in a community that does not have the group best suited for you (Cocaine Anonymous, for example, is difficult to find in rural areas), attend one of the others. The important thing is that you, your family, and your addicted parent attend a group, get a sponsor, and work the program.

It is very important that the addict and his or her family regularly attend a self-help group.

White-Knuckle Sobriety

Sometimes an addict decides to quit using a mood-altering chemical on his own. The addict intends to do so by the strength of his own willpower and is "hanging on to sobriety until his knuckles turn white." That never works!

The first of the twelve steps is the addict's admission of powerlessness over the mood-altering substance or behavior. When an addict tries to achieve recovery by his own power, all he gets is sobriety—not recovery.

This is sometimes called "dry drunk syndrome," because although the addict has quit using, all of the addictive defenses are still in place. In other words, the addict still has an addicted personality even though he is not practicing the addiction.

At Alateen meetings you may hear a depressed kid say, "Well, Dad has quit drinking, but it sure hasn't changed the way he acts. He's still a monster around the house, yelling at all of us . . . " Almost certainly that kid now has a dry drunk for a father. People in recovery are fun to be around. Dad is hanging on so tight that his knuckles have turned white.

Most dry drunks eventually begin practicing their addiction again. Those who don't are usually miserable for the rest of their lives, or until they let go and get into recovery—and so are their families.

What If Your Drug–Abusing Parent Won't Get Help?

If you have tried everything and your parent or parents refuse to get help, get help for yourself. Attend Children of Alcoholics or Alateen. You can work on your own recovery even if your parent won't work on his or hers. It won't be easy. You may even be forbidden to go "because it will make someone think we have a problem in this family and we don't!" But it can be done.

Read about children of alcoholics. There are many books on the topic that can be very helpful to you (see the list in the back of this book for a place to start). You will learn that other kids growing up with an addicted parent feel and think much the way you do.

That in itself can be healing to you. One of the problems of trying to cope with an addicted parent is the emotional isolation, the feeling of being alone, of being the only kid in the world who has ever had to deal with something like that.

Make an appointment with your school counselor to talk about your parent's addiction and how it is affecting you. More and more school counselors are aware of these issues and have been trained to help.

Go back and read Chapter 13 again. Then apply it to your life. It will help you in your continuing struggle.

For Further Reading

Ackerman, Robert J. *Children of Alcoholics*. Holmes Beach, FL: Learning Publications, 1983.

——. *Growing in the Shadow*. Pompano Beach, FL: Health Communications, 1986.

Anonymous. *The Twelve Steps*. San Diego: Recovery Publications, 1987.

Black, Claudia. *It Will Never Happen to Me*. MAC, 1982.

Dulfano, Celia. *Families, Alcoholism, and Recovery*. Minneapolis: Hazelden, 1982.

Gravits, Herbert L., and Bowden, Julie D. *Guide to Recovery*. Holmes Beach, FL: Learning Publications, 1985.

Kathleen, W., and Jewell, E. *With Gentleness, Humor and Love*. Deerfield Beach, FL: Health Communications. 1989.

Larsen, Erie. *Old Patterns, New Truths*. New York: Harper/Hazelden, 1988.

Leite, Evelyn, and Espeland, Pamela. *Different Like Me*. Minneapolis: Johnson Institute, 1987.

Porterfield, Marie Porter. *Coping with an Alcoholic Parent*, rev.ed. New York: Rosen Publishing Group, 1990.

Subby, Robert. *Lost in the Shuffle*. Deerfield Beach, FL: Health Communications, 1987.

Van Nostrand, Randy. *Healing Hearts*. Tulsa, OK: New Choice, 1991.

Wegscheider, Sharon. *Another Chance: Hope and Help for the Alcoholic Family*. Palo Alto, CA: Science and Behavior Books, 1983.

——. *Learning to Love Yourself*. Deerfield Beach, FL: Health Communications, 1987.

———. *The Miracle of Recovery*. Deerfield Beach, FL: Health Communications, 1989.

Woititz, Janet G. *Adult Children of Alcoholics*. Hollywood, FL: Health Communications, 1983.

Index